GUITAR CHORDS Deluxe

INTRODUCTION

Guitar Chords Deluxe is designed to serve two purposes: first, it's a reference guide to chords; second, it's a collection of popular guitar sounds.

Use it when you're learning a new song and you come across a chord that's unfamiliar to you. Use it when you're composing your own music and looking for "just the right chord." Use it to explore the guitar fretboard, to improve your chord playing, to increase your understanding of chord theory, or just to discover new and unusual sounds. The applications are almost limitless.

Guitar Chords Deluxe is a superb source for chords, for all playing styles and levels. It contains five easy-to-play voicings of 28 chord qualities for each of the twelve musical keys. All totaled, that's 1,680 chords at your fingertips! These chords and their fingerings have been chosen for their playability and their practicality, ensuring a wealth of usable fingerings for any musical situation.

Enjoy!

CONTENTS

ISBN 978-0-634-07389-2

HAL•LEONARD®
CORPORATION

7777 W. BLUEMOUND RD. P.O. BOX 13819 MILWAUKEE, WI 53213

Copyright © 2004 by HAL LEONARD CORPORATION
International Copyright Secured   All Rights Reserved

For all works contained herein:
Unauthorized copying, arranging, adapting, recording or public performance is an infringement of copyright.
Infringers are liable under the law.

Visit Hal Leonard Online at www.halleonard.com

P9-BYJ-279

HOW TO USE THIS BOOK

Guitar Chords Deluxe contains 1,680 chord voicings and over 330 unique chord types. To help you find your way to the chord you need, all the chords are organized first by root (C, C♯, D, E♭, E, etc.) and then by quality or type (major, minor, seventh, etc.)

Each chord is identified by its symbol: **Csus4**

By its full name: **C suspended fourth**

And by its spelling:

Then, you are given a choice of five voicings, which are presented in chord frames and photos. In a chord frame, the six vertical lines represent the six strings on the guitar, from low E to high E, moving left to right. The horizontal lines represent the frets.

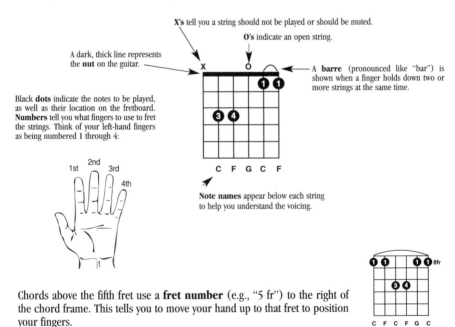

X's tell you a string should not be played or should be muted.

O's indicate an open string.

A dark, thick line represents the **nut** on the guitar.

A **barre** (pronounced like "bar") is shown when a finger holds down two or more strings at the same time.

Black **dots** indicate the notes to be played, as well as their location on the fretboard. **Numbers** tell you what fingers to use to fret the strings. Think of your left-hand fingers as being numbered 1 through 4:

1st 2nd 3rd 4th

Note names appear below each string to help you understand the voicing.

Chords above the fifth fret use a **fret number** (e.g., "5 fr") to the right of the chord frame. This tells you to move your hand up to that fret to position your fingers.

One of the goals of this book is to provide "playable" chord fingerings. The fingerings in this book were chosen for their ease of play and transition between other chords in a progression. However, remember that they are only recommended fingerings. If you feel more comfortable with an alternate fingering, feel free to use it.

CHOOSING THE BEST VOICING

Any chord can have a number of different voicings. A *voicing* refers to how the notes of the chord are arranged—which corresponds to where the chord is played on the guitar, and how it's fingered. Each chord quality in this book is presented with *five* different voicings. Typically, the first chord voicing presented is in the lowest position on the fretboard. The rest of the voicings gradually move up the neck. Within these sets of voicings, you will encounter open chords, barre chords, broken-set chords, and adjacent-set chords:

open strings

OPEN CHORDS

Open chords occur within the first five frets of the guitar and contain at least one open string. These chords are often the most appropriate choice for strumming purposes. They're also typically the easiest voicings to learn when you're a beginner.

BARRE CHORDS

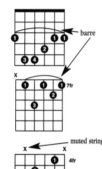

barre

Barre chords can occur anywhere on the neck and serve as a type of "all-purpose" chord voicing; that is, they can be strummed, plucked, or played fingerstyle, and can be used in almost any musical setting.

Barre chords require you to lay a finger flat across a fret and press down all the indicated strings simultaneously. This can be challenging for a beginning guitarist. If you find these chords to be especially difficult at first, don't give up. Just keep practicing, and be patient.

BROKEN-SET CHORDS

muted string

Broken-set chords also provide good, multipurpose chord voicings. These chords contain a bass note on the fifth or sixth string and two or three notes on the higher strings, with at least one interior string muted, or not played. These often work best in a jazz or blues setting, especially when playing solo.

ADJACENT-SET CHORDS

Adjacent-set chords contain notes on the middle or top four strings. These chords also work well within the jazz or blues idioms, especially for chord-melody techniques or when playing with another instrument that provides a bass line.

One thing to remember is that many of these voicings are unique. Open strings are taken advantage of when possible, but many moveable voicings are included as well. So, just because you've learned two moveable shapes for C7, for example, that doesn't mean there aren't any more moveable seventh chord shapes in the book. Usually, you'll find other moveable voicings for the same chord by looking through the other keys throughout the book.

Ultimately, which chord voicing you choose will depend on either your playing level or the situation at hand. Musically speaking, if you're playing a chord sequence high on the neck, a chord voiced down low would probably sound out of place. Likewise, if you're playing a progression of open chords, jumping up high on the neck for a particular chord would likely sound and feel awkward.

That said, you should become familiar with as many voicings of a chord as you can. They do not all sound the same. Practice switching between different voicings of the same chord, and compare how they sound. If you like, go ahead and practice a progression where you jump from high to low on the neck—there really are no rules in music that can't be broken.

CHORD CONSTRUCTION

WHAT'S A CHORD?

In order to effectively choose and utilize the chords in this book, it is important to have a basic understanding of how chords are constructed. So, *what is a chord?* A chord is simply defined as *three or more notes* played at the same time. Typically, its function is to provide the harmony that supports the melody of a song.

HOW DOES A CHORD GET ITS NAME?

A chord gets its name from its root note. For example, the root of a G major chord is G. The remaining notes in the chord determine its *quality,* or *type.* This is indicated by the chord suffix. So, in a Bm7♭5 chord, B is the root, and m7♭5 is the suffix that indicates the quality of the chord.

root

quality or type

This book contains 28 chord types. Here is a summary table to help you keep track of the suffix for each chord type:

SUFFIX	CHORD TYPE	SUFFIX	CHORD TYPE
no suffix	major	m(maj7)	minor, major seventh
5(no 3rd)	fifth (power chord)	m9	minor ninth
sus4	suspended fourth	m11	minor eleventh
sus2	suspended second	7	dominant seventh
add9	added ninth	7sus4	seventh, suspended fourth
6	sixth	7♭5	seventh, flat fifth
maj7	major seventh	9	ninth
maj9	major ninth	7♯9	seventh, sharp ninth
maj7♯11	major seventh, sharp eleventh	11	eleventh
m	minor	13	thirteenth
m(add9)	minor, added ninth	+	augmented
m6	minor sixth	+7	seventh, sharp fifth
m7	minor seventh	°	diminished
m7♭5	minor seventh, flat fifth	°7	diminished seventh

HOW DO I BUILD A CHORD?

All chords are constructed using intervals. An interval is the distance between any two notes. Though there are many types of intervals, there are only five categories: *major, minor, perfect, augmented,* and *diminished.* Interestingly, the major scale contains only major and perfect intervals:

The major scale also happens to be a great starting point from which to construct chords. For example, if we start at the root (C) and add the interval of a major third (E) and a perfect fifth (G), we have constructed a C major chord.

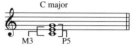

In order to construct a chord other than a major chord, at least one of the major or perfect intervals needs to be altered. For example, take the C major chord you just constructed, and lower the third degree (E) one half step. We now have a C minor chord: C-E♭-G. By lowering the major third by one half step, we create a new interval called a *minor* third.

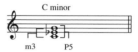

We can further alter the chord by flatting the perfect fifth (G). The chord is now a C°: C-E♭-G♭. The G♭ represents a *diminished* fifth interval.

This leads us to a basic rule of thumb to help remember interval alterations:

A major interval lowered one half step is a minor interval.

A perfect interval lowered one half step is a diminished interval.

A perfect interval raised one half step is an augmented interval.

Half steps and whole steps are the building blocks of intervals; they determine an interval's quality—major, minor, etc. On the guitar, a *half step* is just the distance from one fret to the next. A *whole step* is equal to two half steps, or two frets.

WHAT ABOUT OTHER KEYS?

Notice that we assigned a numerical value to each note in the major scale, as well as labeling the intervals. These numerical values, termed *scale degrees,* allow us to "generically" construct chords, regardless of key. For example, a major chord consists of the root (1), major third (3), and perfect fifth (5). Substitute any major scale for the C major scale above, select scale degrees 1, 3, and 5, and you will have a major chord for the scale you selected.

The chart below is a construction summary of the chord types in this book (based on the key of C only) using the scale degree method:

CHORD TYPE	FORMULA	NOTES	CHORD NAME
major	1-3-5	C-E-G	C
fifth (power chord)	1-5	C-G	C5
suspended fourth	1-4-5	C-F-G	Csus4
suspended second	1-2-5	C-D-G	Csus2
added ninth	1-3-5-9	C-E-G-D	Cadd9
sixth	1-3-5-6	C-E-G-A	C6
major seventh	1-3-5-7	C-E-G-B	Cmaj7
major ninth	1-3-5-7-9	C-E-G-B-D	Cmaj9
major seventh, sharp eleventh	1-3-5-7-♯11	C-E-G-B-F♯	Cmaj7♯11
minor	1-♭3-5	C-E♭-G	Cm
minor, added ninth	1-♭3-5-9	C-E♭-G-D	Cm(add9)
minor sixth	1-♭3-5-6	C-E♭-G-A	Cm6
minor seventh	1-♭3-5-♭7	C-E♭-G-B♭	Cm7
minor seventh, flat fifth	1-♭3-♭5-♭7	C-E♭-G♭-B♭	Cm7♭5
minor, major seventh	1-♭3-5-7	C-E♭-G-B	Cm(maj7)
minor ninth	1-♭3-5-♭7-9	C-E♭-G-B♭-D	Cm9
minor eleventh	1-♭3-5-♭7-9-11	C-E♭-G-B♭-D-F	Cm11
dominant seventh	1-3-5-♭7	C-E-G-B♭	C7
seventh, suspended fourth	1-4-5-♭7	C-F-G-B♭	C7sus4
seventh, flat fifth	1-3-♭5-♭7	C-E-G♭-B♭	C7♭5
ninth	1-3-5-♭7-9	C-E-G-B♭-D	C9
seventh, sharp ninth	1-3-5-♭7-♯9	C-E-G-B♭-D♯	C7♯9
eleventh	1-5-♭7-9-11	C-G-B♭-D-F	C11
thirteenth	1-3-5-♭7-9-13	C-E-G-B♭-D-A	C13
augmented	1-3-♯5	C-E-G♯	C+
seventh, sharp fifth	1-3-♯5-♭7	C-E-G♯-B♭	C+7
diminished	1-♭3-♭5	C-E♭-G♭	C°
diminished seventh	1-♭3-♭5-♭♭7	C-E♭-G♭-B♭♭	C°7

TRIADS

The most basic chords in this book are called triads. A *triad* is a chord that is made up of only three notes. For example, a simple G major chord is a triad consisting of the notes G, B, and D. There are several types of triads, including major, minor, diminished, augmented, and suspended. All of these chords are constructed by simply altering the relationships between the root note and the intervals.

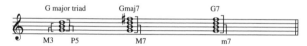

SEVENTHS

To create more interesting harmony, we can take the familiar triad and add another interval: the seventh. Seventh chords are comprised of four notes: the three notes of the triad plus a major or minor seventh interval. For example, if we use the G major triad (G-B-D) and add a major seventh interval (F♯), the Gmaj7 chord is formed. Likewise, if we substitute the minor seventh interval (F) for the F♯, we have a new seventh chord, the G7. This is also known as a dominant seventh chord, popularly used in blues and jazz music. As with the triads, seventh chords come in many types, including major, minor, diminished, augmented, suspended, and others.

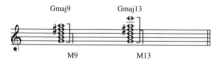

EXTENDED CHORDS

Extended chords are those that include notes beyond the seventh scale degree. These chords have a rich, complex harmony that is very common in jazz music. These include ninths, elevenths, and thirteenth chords. For example, if we take a Gmaj7 chord and add a major ninth interval (A), we get a Gmaj9 chord (G-B-D-F♯-A). We can then add an additional interval, a major thirteenth (E), to form a Gmaj13 chord (G-B-D-F♯-A-E). Note that the interval of a major eleventh is omitted. This is because the major eleventh sonically conflicts with the major third interval, creating a dissonance.

By the way, you may have noticed that these last two chords, Gmaj9 and Gmaj13, contain five and six notes, respectively; however, we only have four fingers in the left hand! Since the use of a barre chord or open-string chord is not always possible, we often need to choose the four notes of the chord that are most important to play. The harmonic theory that underlies these choices is beyond the scope of this book, but do not worry—it has already been done for you where necessary. Below are two examples to demonstrate these chord "trimmings."

Generally speaking, the root, third, and seventh are the most crucial notes to include in an extended chord, along with the uppermost extension (ninth, thirteenth, etc.).

INVERSIONS & VOICINGS

This brings us to our last topic. Though a typical chord might consist of only three or four notes—a C triad, for example, consists of just a root, third, and fifth; a G7 chord consists of a root, third, fifth, and seventh—these notes do not necessarily have to appear in that same order, from bottom to top, in the actual chords you play. Inversions are produced when you rearrange the notes of a chord:

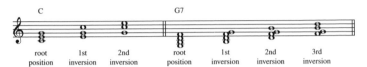

C			G7			
root position	1st inversion	2nd inversion	root position	1st inversion	2nd inversion	3rd inversion

Practically speaking, on the guitar, notes of a chord are often inverted (rearranged), doubled (used more than once), and even omitted to create different voicings. Each voicing is unique and yet similar—kind of like different shades of the same color.

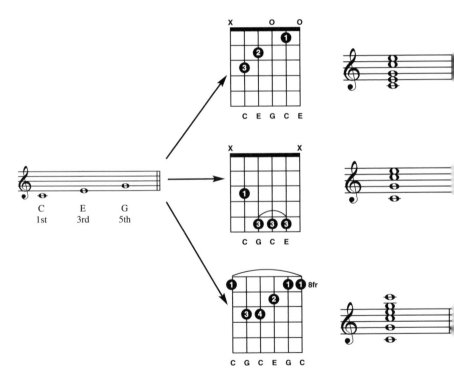

Once again, the possible voicings of a chord are many. The voicings in this book were chosen because they are some of the most popular, useful, and attractive chord voicings playable on the guitar.

C (Cmaj)
major

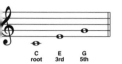

C root   E 3rd   G 5th

C5 (C no 3rd)
C fifth (power chord)

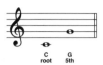

C root   G 5th

C E G C E

G C

C G C E

C G C

5fr

C E G C E

5fr

G C G C

8fr

C G C E G C

8fr

C G C

12fr

E G C

10fr

C G C

Csus4 (Csus)
C suspended fourth

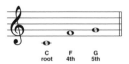

C root | F 4th | G 5th

C F G C F

3fr
G C G C F

5fr
G C F C

8fr
C F C F G C

10fr
C G C F

Csus2 (C5add2)
C suspended second

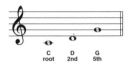

C root | D 2nd | G 5th

C D G C G

3fr
C G D

5fr
D G C G C

7fr
C D G D

D G D G C

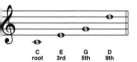

Cadd9
C added ninth

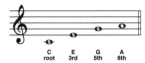

C6
C sixth

Cadd9 notes: C root, E 3rd, G 5th, D 9th

C6 notes: C root, E 3rd, G 5th, A 6th

Cadd9 fingerings:
- C E G D G (X O)
- C G D E G (X, 3fr)
- D G C E (X, X, 5fr)
- E D G C (X, X, 7fr)
- C G C D (X, X, 10fr)

C6 fingerings:
- C E A C E (X O)
- C G C E A (X)
- C A E G (X, X, 7fr)
- C E A C (X, X, 8fr)
- A G C E (X, X, 12fr)

3

Cmaj7 (CM7)
C major seventh

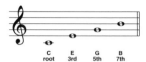

C	E	G	B
root	3rd	5th	7th

C E G B E

C G B E G

5fr

G C E B

8fr

C B E G

10fr

C G B E

Cmaj9 (CM9)
C major ninth

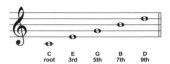

C	E	G	B	D
root	3rd	5th	7th	9th

C E B D

7fr

E B D G B

9f

C E B D

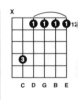
12

C D G B E

14

B E B D G

Cmaj7#11 (CM7#11)
C major seventh, sharp eleventh

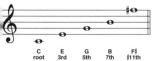

C	E	G	B	F#
root	3rd	5th	7th	#11th

Cm (Cmin, C-)
C minor

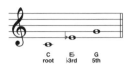

C	Eb	G
root	b3rd	5th

C E G B F#

C Eb G C

C F# B E G

C G C Eb G

4fr

F# C E B

8fr

C G C Eb G C

7fr

C B E F#

10fr

Eb C G C

10fr

C F# B E

11fr

Eb G C Eb

Cm(add9)
C minor, added ninth

C root   E♭ ♭3rd   G 5th   D 9th

C E♭ G D G

E♭ G C D   3fr

E♭ D G C   6fr

C E♭ G D   8fr

D G C E♭   11fr

Cm6 (Cmin6, C-6)
C minor sixth

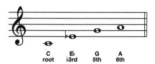

C root   E♭ ♭3rd   G 5th   A 6th

C E♭ A C G

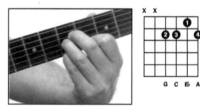

G C E♭ A   4fr

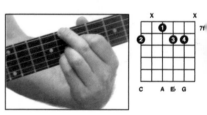

C A E♭ G   7fr

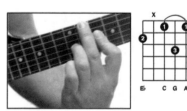

E♭ C G A   10fr

E♭ A C G   13fr

Cm7 (Cmin7, C-7)
C minor seventh

C	E♭	G	B♭
root	♭3rd	5th	♭7th

Cm7♭5 (C-7(♭5), Cmin7-5)
C minor seventh, flat fifth

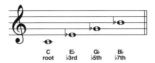

C	E♭	G♭	B♭
root	♭3rd	♭5th	♭7th

G E♭ B♭ C

G♭ E♭ B♭ C

C G B♭ E♭ G

C G♭ B♭ E♭

8fr

C B♭ E♭ G

5fr

E♭ B♭ C G♭

10fr

E♭ C G B♭

7fr

C B♭ E♭ G♭

10fr

C G B♭ E♭

10fr

C G♭ B♭ E♭

10fr

C G B♭ E♭

Cm(maj7) (Cm(+7))
C minor, major seventh

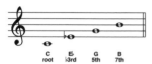

C	Eb	G	B
root	b3rd	5th	7th

X O O

X

C G B Eb G

X   X   8fr

C   B Eb G

X   X   10fr

Eb   C G B

X   X   12fr

B Eb G C

Cm9 (Cmin9, C-9)
C minor ninth

C	Eb	G	Bb	D
root	b3rd	5th	b7th	9th

X

C Eb Bb D G

X   X   6fr

Eb   D G B Bb

       8fr

C G Bb Eb G D

X X   8fr

C Eb Bb D

X X   1

Eb Bb D G

C

Cm11 (C-11, Cmin11)
C minor eleventh

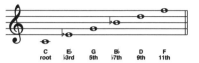

C	E♭	G	B♭	D	F
root	♭3rd	5th	♭7th	9th	11th

C7 (Cdom7)
C dominant seventh

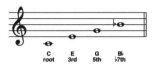

C	E	G	B♭
root	3rd	5th	♭7th

C E♭ B♭ C F

C E B♭ C E

C F B♭ E♭ G

C G B♭ E G

6fr

C B♭ E♭ F

5fr

G C E B♭

10fr

C F B♭ E♭

8fr

C G B♭ E G C

13fr

C B♭ E♭ F

10fr

C G B♭ E

C7sus4 (C7sus)
C dominant seventh, suspended fourth

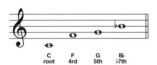

C	F	G	B♭
root	4rd	5th	♭7th

C F B♭ C

C G B♭ F G — 3fr

G C F B♭ — 5fr

C G B♭ F G C — 8fr

C G B♭ F — 10fr

C7♭5 (C7-5, Cdom7♭5)
C dominant seventh, flat fifth

C	E	G♭	B♭
root	3rd	♭5th	♭7th

G♭ E B♭ C

C G♭ B♭ E

B♭ G♭ C E — 4fr

C B♭ E G♭ — 7fr

C G♭ B♭ E — 10fr

C

C9
C ninth

C	E	G	B♭	D
root	3rd	5th	♭7th	9th

C7♯9 (C7+9, Cdom7♯9)
C dominant seventh, sharp ninth

C	E	G	B♭	D♯
root	3rd	5th	♭7th	♯9th

C E B♭ D G

C E B♭ D♯

5fr

C B♭ D E

7fr

E B♭ D♯ G C

7fr

E B♭ D G

8fr

C G B♭ E G D♯

8fr

C G B♭ E G D

9fr

C E B♭ D♯

9fr

C E B♭ D

11fr

D♯ G B♭ E

C11
C eleventh

C	E	G	B♭	D	F
root	3rd	5th	♭7th	9th	11th

C E B♭ C F

C F B♭ E G

5fr

E C F B♭

10fr

C F B♭ E

13fr

F B♭ E B♭ C F

C13 (Cdom13)
C thirteenth

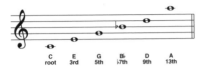

C	E	G	B♭	D	A
root	3rd	5th	♭7th	9th	13th

B♭ E A C

C E B♭ D A

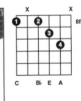

8fr

C B♭ E A

8fr

C G B♭ E A C

13fr

E B♭ C A

C+ (Caug, C(♯5))
C augmented

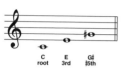

C root   E 3rd   G♯ ♯5th

C+7 (C7♯5)
C dominant seventh, sharp fifth

C root   E 3rd   G♯ ♯5th   B♭ ♭7th

C E G♯ C

E B♭ C G♯

C   C E G♯

3fr

C G♯ B♭ E G♯

5fr

G♯ C E C

5fr

B♭   G♯ C E

8fr

C E G♯ C

8fr

C   B♭ E G♯

12fr

E   E G♯ C

10fr

C G♯ B♭ E

C° (C dim)
C diminished

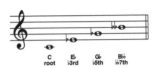

C root E♭ ♭3rd G♭ ♭5th

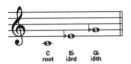

C°7 (Cdim7)
C diminished seventh

C root E♭ ♭3rd G♭ ♭5th B♭♭ ♭♭7th

C# (C#maj)
C-sharp major

C#	E#	G#
root	3rd	5th

C# E# G# C# E#

4fr

C# G# C# E#

6fr

C# E# G# C# E#

9fr

C# G# C# E# G# C#

11fr

C# G# C# E#

C#5 (C# no 3rd)
C-sharp fifth (power chord)

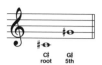

C#	G#
root	5th

C#

G# C# G#

4fr

C# G# C#

6fr

G# C# G# C#

9fr

C# G# C#

11fr

C# G# C#

C#sus4 (C#sus)
C-sharp suspended fourth

C#
root

F#
4th

G#
5th

X X X

G# C# F#

X 4fr

C# F# C# F# G#

X X 6fr

G# C# F# C#

9fr

C# F# C# F# G# C#

X X 11fr

C# G# C# F#

C#sus2 (C#5add2)
C-sharp suspended second

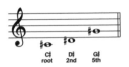

C#
root

D#
2nd

G#
5th

X X X

D# G# C#

X 4fr

C# G# C# D# G#

X 6fr

D# G# C# G# C#

X X X 8fr

C# D# G#

X X 11fr

C# G# C# D#

C#add9
C-sharp added ninth

C# root, E# 3rd, G# 5th, D# 9th

C# E# G# D#

C# G# D# E# — 4fr

D# G# C# E# — 6fr

E# D# G# C# — 8fr

C# E# G# D# — 9fr

C#6
C-sharp sixth

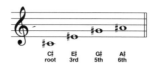

C# root, E# 3rd, G# 5th, A# 6th

A# G# C# E#

C# E# A# C#

C# G# C# E# A# — 4fr

C# A# E# G# — 8fr

C# E# A# C# — 9fr

C#

17

C#maj7 (C#M7)
C-sharp major seventh

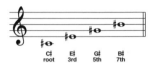

C#	E#	G#	B#
root	3rd	5th	7th

C# E# G# B# E#

C# G# B# E# G#

G# C# E# B#

C# B# E# G#

C# G# B# E#

C#maj9 (C#M9)
C-sharp major ninth

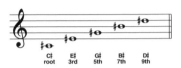

C#	E#	G#	B#	D#
root	3rd	5th	7th	9th

C# D# G# B# E#

C# E# B# D#

G# D# E# B#

E# C# D# G# B#

C# E# B# D#

#maj7#11 (C#M7#11)
-sharp major seventh, sharp eleventh

C#	E#	G#	B#	F×
root	3rd	5th	7th	#11th

C#m (C#m, C#-)
C-sharp minor

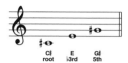

C#	E	G#
root	♭3rd	5th

C#

E# G# B# F×

E G# C# E

C# F× B# E# G#

C# G# C# E G#

 5fr
F× C# E# B#

E G# C# G#

 8fr

C# B# E# F×

C# G# C# E G# C#

 8fr

C# E# F× B#
 11fr

C# G# C# E

C#m(add9)
C-sharp minor, added ninth

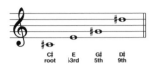

C# E G# D#
root ♭3rd 5th 9th

X X O

D# G# C# E

X X 4fr

E G# C# D#

X X 7fr

E D# G# C#

X X 9fr

C# E G# D#

X X 11fr

E G# C# D#

C#m6 (C#min6, C#-6)
C-sharp minor sixth

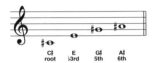

C# E G# A#
root ♭3rd 5th 6th

X

C# E A# C# G#

X X

G# C# E A#

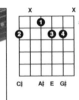

X X

C# A# E G#

C# G# C# E A# C#

X X

C# G# A# E

C#m7 (C#min7, C#-7)
C-sharp minor seventh

C# root   E b3rd   G# 5th   B b7th

C#m7b5 (C#-7(b5), C#min7-5)
C-sharp minor seventh, flat fifth

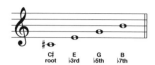

C# root   E b3rd   G b5th   B b7th

X   O O
C# E G# B E

X   O O O
C# E G B E

X   4fr
C# G# B E G#

X   X   4fr
C# G B E

X X   5fr
G# C# E B

X X   6fr
E   C# G B

X   X   9fr
C#   B E G#

X   X   8fr
C#   B E G

X X   11fr
C# G# B E

X X   11fr
C# G B E

C#m(maj7) (C#m(+7))
C-sharp minor, major seventh

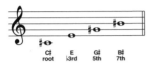

C#	E	G#	B#
root	♭3rd	5th	7th

C# E G# B#

C# G# B# E G#

9fr

C# B# E G#

9fr

B# E G# C#

11fr

C# G# B# E

C#m9 (C#min9, C#-9)
C-sharp minor ninth

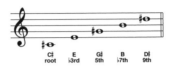

C#	E	G#	B	D#
root	♭3rd	5th	♭7th	9th

C# E B D#

E D# E B

C# G# B E G# D#

C# E B D#

D# G# B E

C#m11 (C#-11, C#min11)
C-sharp minor eleventh

C#	E	G#	B	D#	F#
root	♭3rd	5th	♭7th	9th	11th

C#7 (C#dom7)
C-sharp dominant seventh

C#	E#	G#	B
root	3rd	5th	♭7th

C# E B D# F#

C# E# B C#

C# F# B E G#

E# B C# G#

7fr

E B D# F# C#

4fr

C# G# B E# G#

7fr

C# B E F#

9fr

C# G# B E# G# C#

11fr

C# F# B E

11fr

C# G# B E#

C#7sus4 (C#7sus)
C-sharp dominant seventh, suspended fourth

C# F# G# B
root 4th 5th b7th

X   X

C# F# B C#

X X

F# B C# G#

X

4fr

C# G# B F# G#

9fr

C# G# B F# G# C#

X X

11fr

C# G# B F#

C#7b5 (C#7-5, C#dom7b5)
C-sharp dominant seventh, flat fifth

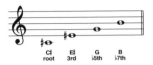

C# E# G B
root 3rd b5th b7th

X   X

G E# B C#

X   X

C# G B E#

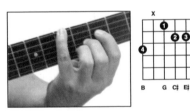

X   X

B G C# E#

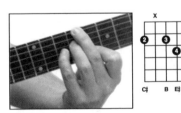

X   X

C# B E# G

X X

C# G B E#

C#9
-sharp ninth

C#	E#	G#	B	D#
root	3rd	5th	♭7th	9th

C#7#9 (C#7+9, C#dom7#9)
C-sharp dominant seventh, sharp ninth

C#	E#	G#	B	D𝄪
root	3rd	5th	♭7th	#9th

C#

C# E# B D# G#

C# E# G# B D𝄪

6fr

C# B D# E#

C# E# B D𝄪

8fr

E# B D# G#

6fr

D𝄪 G# C# E# B

9fr

C# G# B E# G# D#

9fr

C# G# B E# G# D𝄪

10fr

C# E# B D#

12fr

E# G# B D𝄪

C♯11
C-sharp eleventh

C♯	E♯	G♯	B	D♯	F♯
root	3rd	5th	♭7th	9th	11th

C♯13 (C♯dom13)
C-sharp thirteenth

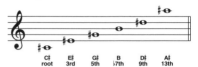

C♯	E♯	G♯	B	D♯	A♯
root	3rd	5th	♭7th	9th	13th

C♯ E♯ B C♯ F♯

B E♯ A♯ C♯

C♯ F♯ B E♯ G♯ — 4fr

C♯ E♯ B D♯ A♯ — 3

C♯ B E♯ F♯ — 7fr

C♯ B D♯ E♯ A♯

F♯ B E♯ G♯ C♯ — 9fr

C♯ G♯ B E♯ A♯ C♯ — 9

C♯ F♯ B E♯ — 11fr

B A♯ C♯ E♯

C#+ (C#aug, C#(#5))
C-sharp augmented

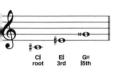

C# — root
E# — 3rd
G𝄪 — #5th

C#+7 (C#7#5)
C-sharp dominant seventh, sharp fifth

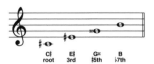

C# — root
E# — 3rd
G𝄪 — #5th
B — ♭7th

C# E# G𝄪 C#

C# E# G𝄪 B E#

4fr

C# C# E# G𝄪

E# B C# G𝄪

6fr

G𝄪 C# E# C#

4fr

C# G𝄪 B E# G𝄪

9fr

C# E# G𝄪 C#

9fr

C# B E# G𝄪

12fr

G𝄪 E# G𝄪 C#

11fr

C# G𝄪 B E#

C#° (C#dim)
C-sharp diminished

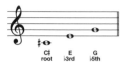

C#   E   G
root   ♭3rd   ♭5th

C#°7 (C#dim7)
C-sharp diminished seventh

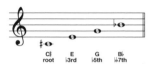

C#   E   G   B♭
root   ♭3rd   ♭5th   ♭♭7th

X   O   O

C# E G C# E

X   O   O

B♭ E G C# E

X   X   3fr

G C# E G

X   X

E B♭ C# G

X   X   8fr

C# E G C#

X   X

C# G B♭ E

X   X   11fr

C# G C# E

X   X   8fr

C# B♭ E G

X   X   12fr

E E G C#

X   X   9fr

E G B♭ C#

D (Dmaj)
D major

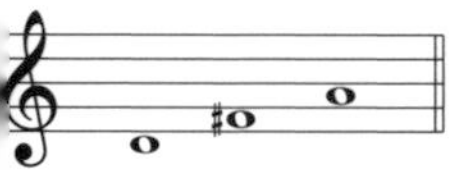
D
root
F♯
3rd
A
5th

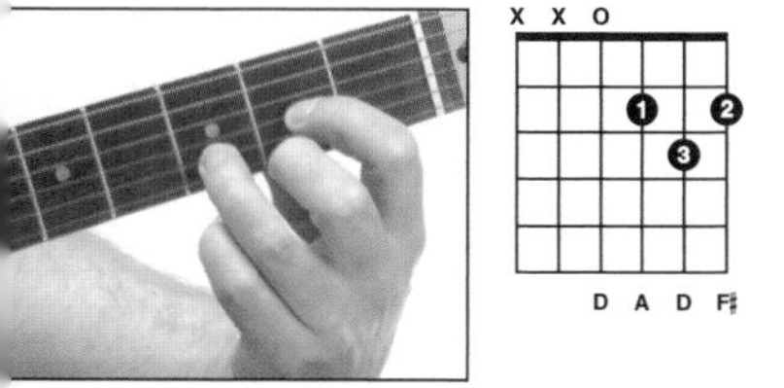
X X O
D A D F♯

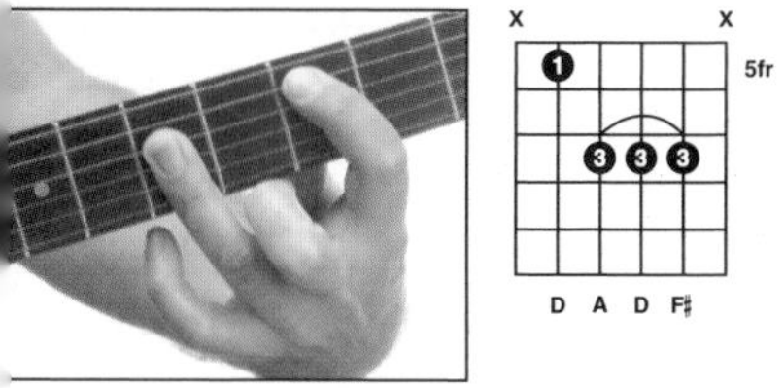
X X
5fr
D A D F♯

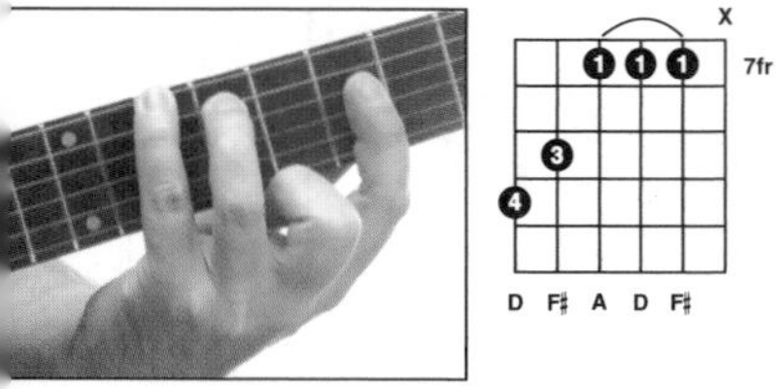
X
7fr
D F♯ A D F♯

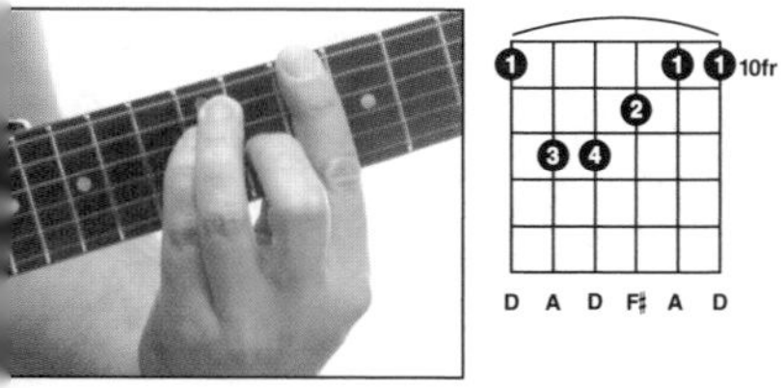
10fr
D A D F♯ A D

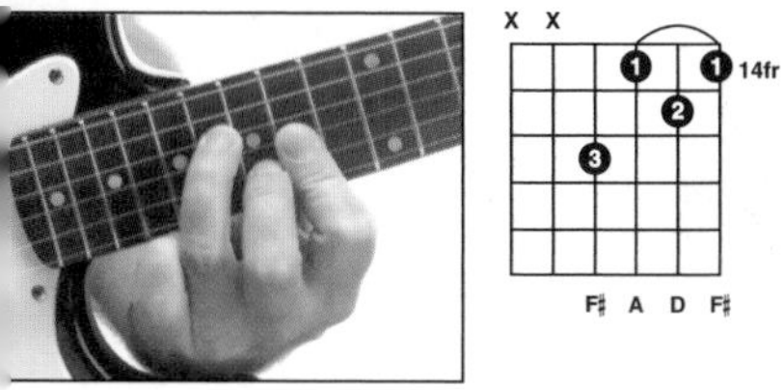
X X
14fr
F♯ A D F♯

D5 (D no 3rd)
D fifth (power chord)

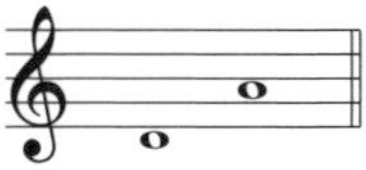
D
root
A
5th

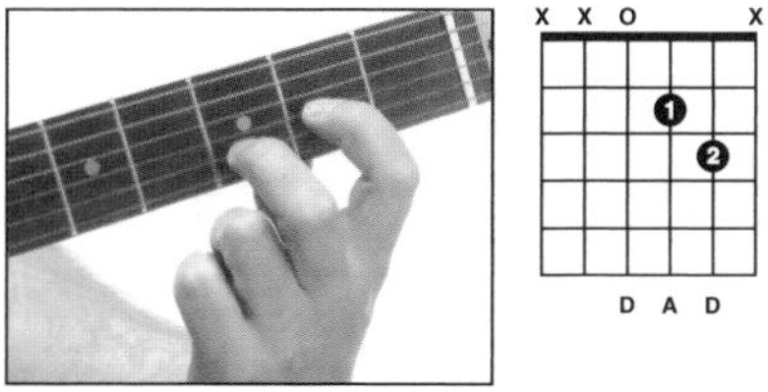
X X O X
D A D

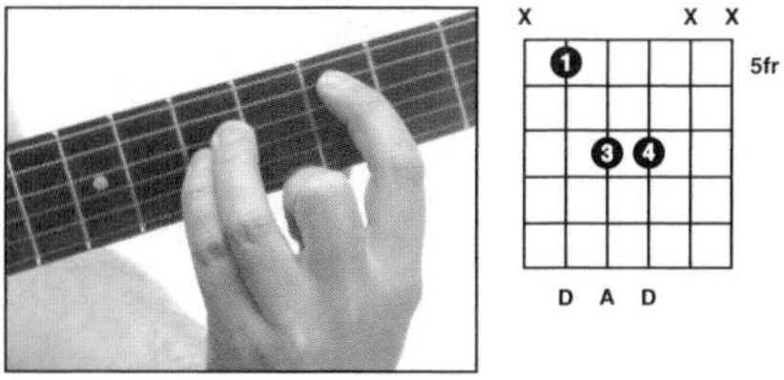
X X X
5fr
D A D

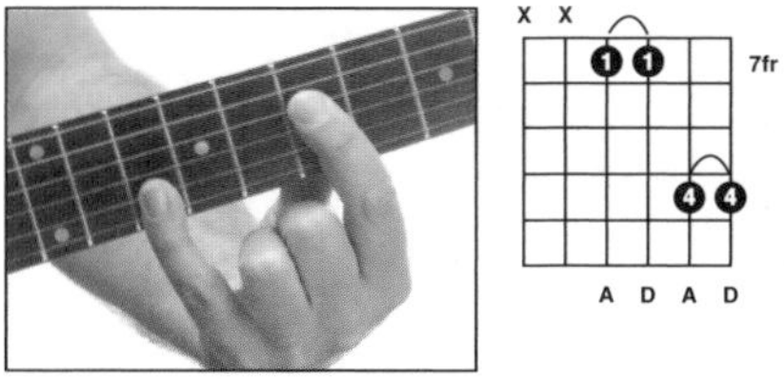
X X
7fr
A D A D

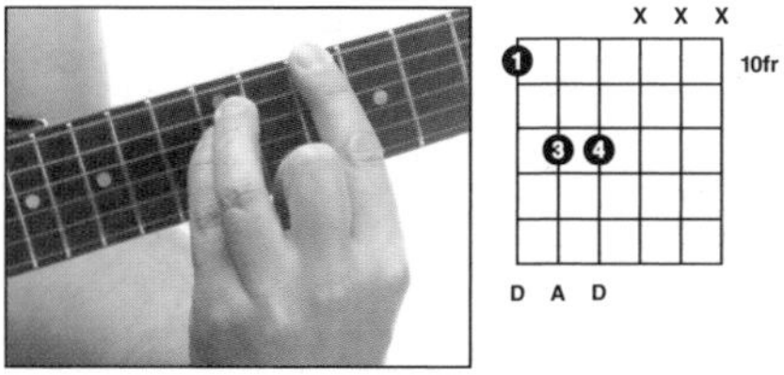
X X X
10fr
D A D

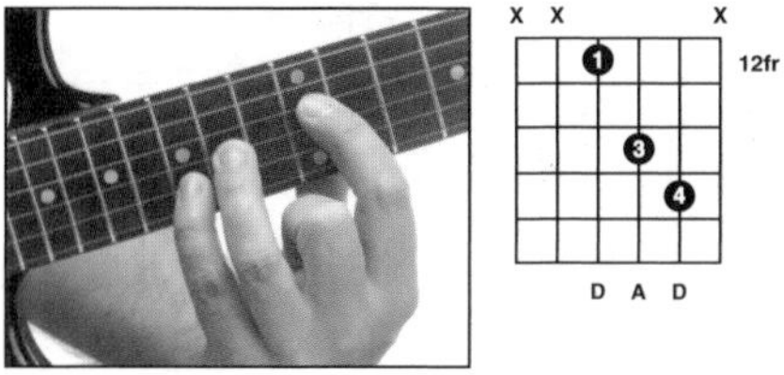
X X X
12fr
D A D

Dsus4 (Dsus)
D suspended fourth

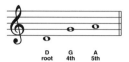

D root   G 4th   A 5th

X X O

D A D G

X   X
5fr

D A D G

X X
7fr

A D G D

10fr

D G D G A D

X
12fr

A D G D G

Dsus2 (D5add2)
D suspended second

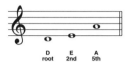

D root   E 2nd   A 5th

X X O   O

D A D E

X
5

D A D E A

X
7

E A E A D

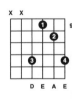

X X
9

D E A E

X
11

A D A D E

add9
added ninth

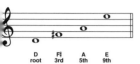

D	F♯	A	E
root	3rd	5th	9th

D6
D sixth

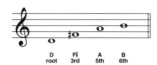

D	F♯	A	B
root	3rd	5th	6th

D

F♯ A D E

D A B F♯

4fr

A F♯ D E

B F♯ A D A

7fr

E A D F♯

5fr

D A D F♯ B

9fr

F♯ E A D

9fr

D B F♯ A

10fr

D F♯ A E

12fr

D A B F♯

Dmaj7 (DM7)
D major seventh

D   F♯   A   C♯
root 3rd 5th 7th

Dmaj9 (DM9)
D major ninth

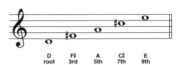

D   F♯   A   C♯   E
root 3rd 5th 7th 9th

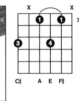

maj7♯11 (DM7♯11)
major seventh, sharp eleventh

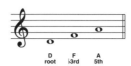

D	F♯	A	C♯	G♯
root	3rd	5th	7th	♯11th

Dm (Dmin, D-)
D minor

D	F	A
root	♭3rd	5th

 — X X O — D G♯ C♯ F♯

 — X X O — D A D F

 — X 4fr — D F♯ C♯ F♯ G♯

 — X 5fr — D A D F A

 — X X 5fr — D G♯ C♯ F♯

 — X X 7fr — A F A D

 — X X 9fr — D C♯ F♯ G♯

 — 10fr — D A D F A D

 — X X 12fr — D G♯ C♯ F♯

 — X X 10fr — D F A F

Dm(add9)
D minor, added ninth

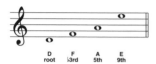

D	F	A	E
root	♭3rd	5th	9th

F A D E

5fr

F A D E

7fr

F A E A D

10fr

D F A E

13fr

E A D F

Dm6 (Dmin6, D-6)
D minor sixth

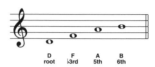

D	F	A	B
root	♭3rd	5th	6th

D A B F

 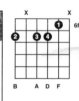

F B D A

6fr

B A D F

9fr

D B F A

12fr

D A B F

m7 (D-7, Dmin7)
minor seventh

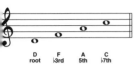

D	F	A	C
root	♭3rd	5th	♭7th

Dm7♭5 (D-7♭5, Dmin7-5)
D minor seventh, flat fifth

D	F	A♭	C
root	♭3rd	♭5th	♭7th

D

X X O

D A C F

X X O

D A♭ C F

X 5fr

D A C F A

X X

A♭ F C D

X X 6fr

A D F C

X X 5fr

D A♭ C F

X X 10fr

D C F A

X X 9fr

D C F A♭

10fr

D A C F C D

X X 12fr

D A♭ C F

Dm(maj7) (D-(+7))
D minor, major seventh

D	F	A	C#
root	♭3rd	5th	7th

D A C# F

D A C# F A

A D F C#

D C# F A

C# F A D

Dm9 (D-9, Dmin9)
D minor ninth

D	F	A	C	E
root	♭3rd	5th	♭7th	9th

F A C E

D F C E

 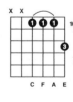

F E A C

C F A E

D A C F C E

Dm11 (D-11, Dmin11)
minor eleventh

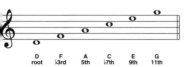

D	F	A	C	E	G
root	♭3rd	5th	♭7th	9th	11th

D7 (Ddom7)
D dominant seventh

D	F♯	A	C
root	3rd	5th	♭7th

D

X X O O
D G C F

X X O
D A C F♯

X
D F C E G

X X
F♯ C D A

X 5fr
D G C F A

X 5fr
D A C F♯ A

X X 8fr
D C F G

10fr
D A C F♯ A D

10fr
D G C F A E

X X 11fr
D F♯ C F♯

D7sus4 (D7sus)
D dominant seventh, suspended fourth

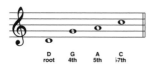

D	G	A	C
root	4th	5th	♭7th

D7♭5 (D7-5, Ddom7♭5)
D dominant seventh, flat fifth

D	F♯	A♭	C
root	3rd	♭5th	♭7th

X X O

D A C G

X X O

D A♭ C F♯

X X

G C D A

X X

F♯ C D A♭

X   5fr

D A C G A

X   X

D A♭ C F♯

X X   7fr

A D G C

X X

A♭ D F♯ C

10fr

D A C G C D

X X

C F♯ A♭ D

9
ninth

D	F♯	A	C	E
root	3rd	5th	♭7th	9th

D7♯9 (D7+9, Ddom7♯9)
D dominant seventh, sharp ninth

D	F♯	A	C	E♯
root	3rd	5th	♭7th	♯9th

D

F♯ A C E

F♯ A C E♯

D F♯ C E A

4fr

D F♯ C E♯

7fr

D C E F♯

7fr

E♯ A D F♯ C

9fr

F♯ C E A

9fr

F♯ C E♯ A D

10fr

D A C F♯ A E

11fr

D F♯ C E♯

D11
D eleventh

D	F#	A	C	E	G
root	3rd	5th	♭7th	9th	11th

D13 (Ddom13)
D thirteenth

D	F#	A	C	E	B
root	3rd	5th	♭7th	9th	13th

X X O O

D G C F#

X O O

A D B C F#

X

D F# C D G

X 3f

C F# B D A

X 5fr

D G C F# A

X 4f

D F# C E B

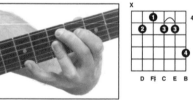

X X 7fr

F# D G C

X 7f

D C E F# B

X X 8fr

D C F# G

10

D A C F# B D

+ (Daug, D(#5))
augmented

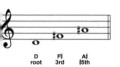

D	F#	A#
root	3rd	#5th

D+7 (D7#5)
D dominant seventh, sharp fifth

D	F#	A#	C
root	3rd	#5th	b7th

X X O

D A# D F#

X X O

D A# C F#

X   X
3fr

D F# A# D

X X
3fr

F# C D A#

X   X
5fr

D   D F# A#

X
5fr

D A# C F# A#

X X
7fr

A# D F# D

X   X
7fr

C A# D F#

X   X
9fr

F# D F# A#

X   X
10fr

D   C F# A#

D° (D dim)
D diminished

D — root
F — ♭3rd
A♭ — ♭5th

D A♭ D F

A♭ D F A♭ (4fr)

F A♭ D A♭ (6fr)

D F A♭ D (9fr)

F A♭ D F (13fr)

D°7 (Ddim7)
D diminished seventh

D — root
F — ♭3rd
A♭ — ♭5th
C♭ — ♭♭7th

D A♭ C♭ F

A♭ F C♭ D (3fr)

D A♭ C♭ F A♭ (4fr)

F A♭ D F C♭ (6fr)

C♭ F A♭ D (7fr)

Eb (Ebmaj)
E-flat major

Eb — root
G — 3rd
Bb — 5th

X X
① ② ③ ④
Eb Bb Eb G

X X
① ② ③ ④ 3fr
Eb G Bb Eb

X X
① ③ ③ ③ 6fr
Eb Bb Eb G

① ① ① ③ ④ 8fr
Eb G Bb Eb G

① ① ① ② ③ ④ 11fr
Eb Bb Eb G Bb Eb

Eb5 (Eb no 3rd)
E-flat fifth (power chord)

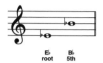

Eb — root
Bb — 5th

X X X
① ③ ④
Eb Bb Eb

X X X
① ③ ④ 6fr
Eb Bb Eb

X X
① ① ④ ④ 8fr
Bb Eb Bb Eb

X X X
① ③ ④ 11fr
Eb Bb Eb

X X X
① ① ③ 13fr
Bb Eb Bb

Eb

E♭sus4 (E♭sus)
E-flat suspended fourth

E♭ root   A♭ 4th   B♭ 5th

E♭sus2 (E♭5add2)
E-flat suspended second

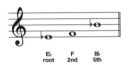

E♭ root   F 2nd   B♭ 5th

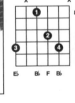

add9
flat added ninth

E♭	G	B♭	F
root	3rd	5th	9th

F B♭ E♭ G

3fr

E♭ G B♭ F

8fr

F B♭ E♭ G

10fr

G F B♭ E♭

11fr

E♭ G B♭ F

E♭6
E-flat sixth

E♭	G	B♭	C
root	3rd	5th	6th

E♭ B♭ C G

3fr

C G B♭ E♭ B♭

6fr

E♭ B♭ E♭ G C

10fr

E♭ C G B♭

11fr

B♭ G C E♭

E♭

E♭maj7 (E♭M7)
E-flat major seventh

E♭	G	B♭	D
root	3rd	5th	7th

E♭ B♭ D G

3fr
E♭ G B♭ D

6fr
E♭ B♭ D G B♭

8fr
B♭ E♭ G D

11fr
E♭ D G B♭

E♭maj9 (E♭M9)
E-flat major ninth

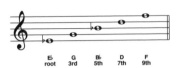

E♭	G	B♭	D	F
root	3rd	5th	7th	9th

E♭ G D F

3fr
E♭ F B♭ D G

5
E♭ G D F

 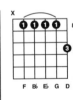

8
F B♭ E♭ G D

E♭ D F G

♭maj7#11 (E♭M7#11)
flat major seventh, sharp eleventh

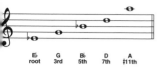

E♭	G	B♭	D	A
root	3rd	5th	7th	#11th

E♭m (E♭min, E♭-)
E-flat minor

E♭	G♭	B♭
root	♭3rd	5th

E♭

E♭ A D G

E♭ B♭ E♭ G♭

5fr

E♭ G D G A

6fr

E♭ B♭ E♭ G♭ B♭

6fr

E♭ A D G

8fr

B♭ G♭ B♭ E♭

8fr

G B♭ E♭ A D

11fr

E♭ B♭ E♭ G♭ B♭ E♭

10fr

E♭ D G A

11fr

E♭ G♭ B♭ G♭

E♭m(add9)
E-flat minor, added ninth

E♭	G♭	B♭	F
root	♭3rd	5th	9th

E♭m6 (E♭min6, E♭-6)
E-flat minor sixth

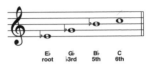

E♭	G♭	B♭	C
root	♭3rd	5th	6th

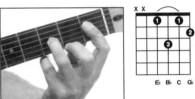

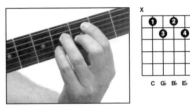

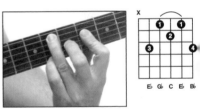

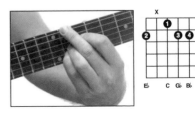

m7 (E♭min7, E♭-7)
flat minor seventh

E♭ — root
G♭ — ♭3rd
B♭ — 5th
D♭ — ♭7th

E♭m7♭5 (E♭-7♭5, E♭min7-5)
E-flat minor seventh, flat fifth

E♭ — root
G♭ — ♭3rd
B♭♭ — ♭5th
D♭ — ♭7th

E♭

E♭ B♭ D♭ G♭

E♭ B♭♭ D♭ G♭

4fr
E♭ G♭ D♭ E♭ B♭

5fr
E♭ D♭ G♭ B♭♭

6fr
E♭ B♭ D♭ G♭ B♭

6fr
E♭ B♭♭ D♭ G♭

11fr
E♭ D♭ G♭ B♭

9fr
E♭ G♭ B♭♭ D♭

11fr
E♭ B♭ D♭ G♭ D♭ E♭

10fr
E♭ D♭ G♭ B♭♭

E♭m(maj7) (E♭-(+7))
E-flat minor, major seventh

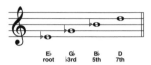

E♭	G♭	B♭	D
root	♭3rd	5th	7th

X X

E♭ B♭ D G♭

X   X   3fr

E♭ G♭ B♭ D

X   6fr

E♭ B♭ D G♭ B♭

X X   7fr

B♭ E♭ G♭ D

X   X   11fr

E♭   D G♭ B♭

E♭m9 (E♭min9, E♭-9)
E-flat minor ninth

E♭	G♭	B♭	D♭	F
root	♭3rd	5th	♭7th	9th

X X

G♭ B♭ D♭ F

X   X

E♭ G♭ D♭ F

X   X

F   D♭ G♭ B♭

X X

D♭ G♭ B♭ F

E♭ B♭ D♭ G♭ D♭ F

m11 (E♭-11, E♭min11)
flat minor eleventh

E♭	G♭	B♭	D♭	F	A♭
root	♭3rd	5th	♭7th	9th	11th

E♭7 (E♭dom7)
E-flat dominant seventh

E♭	G	B♭	D♭
root	3rd	5th	♭7th

E♭

X X

E♭ A♭ D♭ G♭

X X

E♭ B♭ D♭ G

X 4fr

E♭ G♭ D♭ F A♭

X X 3fr

D♭ B♭ E♭ G

X 6fr

E♭ A♭ D♭ G♭ B♭

X X 4fr

E♭ G D♭ E♭

X X 9fr

E♭ D♭ G♭ A♭

X 6fr

E♭ B♭ D♭ G B♭

11fr

E♭ A♭ D♭ G♭ B♭ F

X 11fr

E♭ B♭ D♭ G D♭ E♭

E♭7sus4 (E♭7sus)
E-flat dominant seventh, suspended fourth

E♭ root / A♭ 4th / B♭ 5th / D♭ ♭7th

E♭7♭5 (E♭7-5, E♭dom7♭5)
E-flat dominant seventh, flat fifth

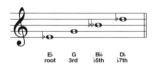

E♭ root / G 3rd / B♭♭ ♭5th / D♭ ♭7th

E♭ B♭ D♭ A♭

E♭ B♭♭ D♭ G

A♭ D♭ E♭ B♭ — 4fr

G D♭ E♭ B♭♭

E♭ B♭ D♭ A♭ B♭ — 6fr

E♭ B♭♭ D♭ G

B♭ E♭ A♭ D♭ — 8fr

B♭♭ E♭ G D♭

E♭ B♭ D♭ A♭ D♭ E♭ — 11fr

E♭ D♭ G B♭♭

♭9
lat ninth

E♭	G	B♭	D♭	F
root	3rd	5th	♭7th	9th

E♭7♯9 (E♭7+9, E♭dom7♯9)
E-flat dominant seventh, sharp ninth

E♭	G	B♭	D♭	F♯
root	3rd	5th	♭7th	♯9th

X X O

E♭ G D♭ F

X X O

E♭ G D♭ F♯

X 5fr

E♭ G D♭ F B♭

X X

F♯ B♭ D♭ G

X X 6fr

F D♭ G B♭

X X 5fr

E♭ G D♭ F♯

X X 8fr

E♭ D♭ F G

X 10fr

G D♭ F♯ B♭ E♭

X X 11fr

E♭ B♭ D♭ G B♭ F

X 11fr

E♭ B♭ D♭ G B♭ F♯

E♭11
E-flat eleventh

E♭	G	B♭	D♭	F	A♭
root	3rd	5th	♭7th	9th	11th

E♭ A♭ D♭ G

A♭ D♭ G D♭ E♭ A♭ 4fr

E♭ G D♭ E♭ A♭ 4fr

E♭ A♭ D♭ G B♭ 6fr

G E♭ A♭ D♭ 8fr

E♭13 (E♭dom13)
E-flat dominant thirteenth

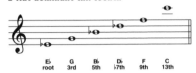

E♭	G	B♭	D♭	F	C
root	3rd	5th	♭7th	9th	13th

C F G D♭

D♭ G C E♭

E♭ G D♭ F

D♭ E♭ G

E♭ D♭ G C

+ (E♭aug, E♭(♯5))
E♭ flat augmented

E♭	G	B
root	3rd	♯5th

E♭+7 (E♭7♯5)
E-flat dominant seventh, sharp fifth

E♭	G	B	D♭
root	3rd	♯5th	♭7th

E♭

X X O O

E♭ G B G

X O

B E♭ G D♭ G

X X

G B E♭ G

X X 2fr

E♭ G B D♭

X X 4fr

E♭ G B E♭

X X 6fr

E♭ B D♭ G B

X X 6fr

E♭ E♭ G B

X X 8fr

D♭ B E♭ G

X X 8fr

B E♭ G E♭

X X 11fr

E♭ D♭ G B

E♭° (E♭dim)
E-flat diminished

E♭   G♭   B♭♭
root   ♭3rd   ♭5th

E♭°7 (E♭dim7)
E-flat diminished seventh

E♭   G♭   B♭♭   D♭♭
root   ♭3rd   ♭5th   ♭♭7th

(Emaj)
major

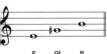

E	G♯	B
root	3rd	5th

E5 (E no 3rd)
E fifth (power chord)

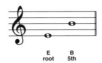

E	B
root	5th

E B E G♯ B E

E B E

G♯ B E G♯

E B E

E B E G♯

E B E

E G♯ B E G♯

B E B E

E B E G♯ B E

E B E

Esus4 (Esus)
E suspended fourth

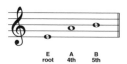

E root · A 4th · B 5th

Esus2 (E5add2)
E suspended second

E root · F♯ 2nd · B 5th

 O O O — E B E A B E

 X X — E B E F♯

 X X — E B E A

 X X — F♯ B E B

 X X 7fr — E B E A

 X — E B E F♯ B

 X X 9fr — B E A E

 X — F♯ B E B E

 12fr — E A E A B E

 X X — E · F♯ B E

add9
added ninth

E6
E sixth

E	G♯	B	F♯
root	3rd	5th	9th

E	G♯	B	C♯
root	3rd	5th	6th

E B E G♯ B F♯

E B E G♯ C♯ E

E

F♯ B E G♯

E B C♯ G♯

6fr

B G♯ E F♯

6fr

E C♯ G♯ B

9fr

F♯ B E G♯

7fr

E B E G♯ C♯

11fr

G♯ F♯ B E

11fr

E C♯ G♯ B

Emaj7 (EM7)
E major seventh

E	G#	B	D#
root	3rd	5th	7th

E B D# G# B E

E B D# G#

7fr

E B D# G# B

11fr

E G# B D#

12fr

E D# G# B

Emaj9 (EM9)
E major ninth

E	G#	B	D#	F#
root	3rd	5th	7th	9th

E B D# G# B F#

E F# B D# G#

E G# D# F#

D# B F# G#

E G# D# F#

maj7#11 (EM7#11)
major seventh, sharp eleventh

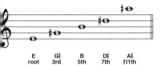

E	G#	B	D#	A#
root	3rd	5th	7th	#11th

Em (Emin, E-)
E minor

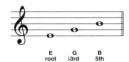

E	G	B
root	♭3rd	5th

E

E B E A# D# G#

E B E G B E

E G# D# G# A# (6fr)

E B E G (X X)

E A# D# G# (7fr)

E B E G B (7fr)

E D# G# A# (11fr)

B G B E (9fr)

E A# D# G# (14fr)

E B E G B E (12fr)

Em(add9)
E minor, added ninth

E	G	B	F#
root	♭3rd	5th	9th

E B E G B F#

F# B E G

F# E G B   7fr

G B F# B E   9fr

E G B F#   12fr

Em6 (Emin6, E-6)
E minor sixth

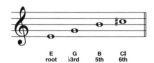

E	G	B	C#
root	♭3rd	5th	6th

E B E G C# E

E B C# G

E G C# E B

C# B E G

E C# G B

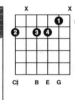

m7 (Emin7, E-7)
minor seventh

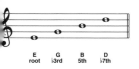

E root / G ♭3rd / B 5th / D ♭7th

O O O

E B E G D E

X X

E B D G

7fr

E B D G B

X X

12fr

E D G B

12fr

E B D G B E

Em7♭5 (E-7♭5, Emin7-5)
E minor seventh, flat fifth

E root / G ♭3rd / B♭ ♭5th / D ♭7th

X X

E B♭ D G

X

5fr

E G D E B♭

X X

7fr

E B♭ D G

X

8fr

G B♭ E G D

X X

11fr

E D G B♭

E

Em(maj7) (E-(+7))
E minor, major seventh

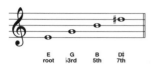

E	G	B	D♯
root	♭3rd	5th	7th

E B D♯ G B E

E B D♯ G

4fr

E G B D♯

7fr

E B D♯ G B

12fr

E D♯ G B

Em9 (Emin9, E-9)
E minor ninth

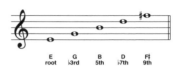

E	G	B	D	F♯
root	♭3rd	5th	♭7th	9th

E B D G B F♯

5

E G D F♯

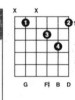

10fr

G F♯ B D

D G B F♯

E B D G D F♯

n11 (E-11, Emin11)
ninor eleventh

E	G	B	D	F♯	A
root	♭3rd	5th	♭7th	9th	11th

o o o o o

E A D G B F♯

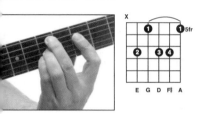

X · · · 5fr

E G D F♯ A

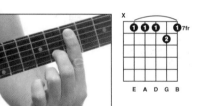

X · · · 7fr

E A D G B

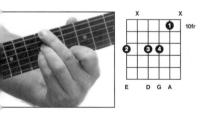

X · · X · 10fr

E D G A

X X · 14fr

E A D G

E7 (Edom7)
E dominant seventh

E	G♯	B	D
root	3rd	5th	♭7th

o o o o

E B D G♯ B E

X X

E B D G♯

X · · 7fr

E B D G♯ B

X · · X 9fr

D B E G♯

· · 12fr

E B D G♯ D E

E7sus4 (E7sus)
E dominant seventh, suspended fourth

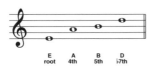

E	A	B	D
root	4th	5th	♭7th

O   O   O O

E B D A B E

x x

E B D A

X   7fr

E B D A B

X   X   9fr

D   B E A

12fr

E B D A D E

E7♭5 (E7-5, Edom7♭5)
E dominant seventh, flat fifth

E	G♯	B♭	D
root	3rd	♭5th	♭7th

x x

E B♭ D G♯

x x

G♯ D E B♭

x   x

E B♭ D G♯

x   x

D   B♭ E G♯

x   x

B♭ E G♯ D

nth

E	G♯	B	D	F♯
root	3rd	5th	♭7th	9th

E7♯9 (E7+9, Edom7♯9)
E dominant seventh, sharp ninth

E	G♯	B	D	F♯✕
root	3rd	5th	♭7th	♯9th

O O O

E B D G♯ B F♯

O O

E B D G♯ D F✕

X

6fr

E G♯ D F♯ B

X X

F✕ B D G♯

X X

9fr

E D F♯ G♯

X X

6fr

E G♯ D F✕

X X

11fr

G♯ D F♯ B

X

11fr

G♯ D F✕ B E

X X

13fr

E G♯ D F♯

12fr

E B D G♯ B F✕

E11
E eleventh

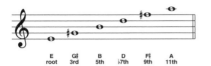

E	G#	B	D	F#	A
root	3rd	5th	♭7th	9th	11th

E A E G# D F#

E A D G#

5fr

E G# D E A

7fr

E A D G# B

10fr

A G# B D

E13 (Edom13)
E thirteenth

E	G#	B	D	F#	C#
root	3rd	5th	♭7th	9th	13th

E B D G# C# F#

D G# C# E

E G# D F# C#

 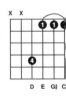

D E G# C

E B D G# C# E

+ (Eaug, E(♯5))
ugmented

E	G♯	B♯
root	3rd	♯5th

E+7 (E7♯5)
E seventh, sharp fifth

E	G♯	B♯	D
root	3rd	♯5th	♭7th

E

X X   O
❶❷
❸

E G♯ B♯ E

X X O   O
❶❷

D G♯ B♯ E

X X
❶   ❷
❸❹

G♯   B♯ E G♯

X X
❶
❷
❸
❹

E B♯ D G♯

X   X
❶❶ 5fr
❷
❸

E G♯ B♯ E

X
❶ ❶ 7fr
❷
❸
❹

E B♯ D G♯ B♯

X   X
❶ 7fr
❷
❸❹

E   E G♯ B♯

X   X
❶❶ 9fr
❷ ❸

D   B♯ E G♯

X X
❶❶ 9fr
❷
❹

B♯ E G♯ E

X   X
❶ ❷ 12fr
❸❹

E   D G♯ B♯

E° (Edim)
E diminished

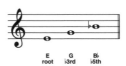

E / root G / ♭3rd B♭ / ♭5th

E°7 (Edim7)
E diminished seventh

E / root G / ♭3rd B♭ / ♭5th D♭ / ♭♭7th

(Fmaj)
major

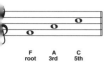

F A C
root 3rd 5th

F5 (F no 3rd))
F fifth (power chord)

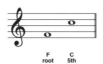

F C
root 5th

F C F A C F

X X X

F C F

X 5fr
F A C F A

X X X 3fr

F C F

X X 8fr
F C F A

X X X 8fr

F C F

X 10fr
F A C F A

X X 10fr

C F C F

X X 13fr
F A C F

X X X 13fr

F C F

F

Fsus4 (Fsus)
F suspended fourth

F	Bb	C
root	4th	5th

F C F Bb C F

X X   3fr

F C F Bb

X   X   5fr

F Bb C F

X   X   8fr

F C F Bb

X X   13fr

F Bb C F

Fsus2 (F5add2)
F suspended second

F	G	C
root	2nd	5th

X X   O

F G C F

X X

F C F G

X   X

F G C F

X

F C F G C

X X

F   G C F

add9
added ninth

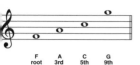

F	A	C	G
root	3rd	5th	9th

F6
F sixth

F	A	C	D
root	3rd	5th	6th

F A C G

F D A C

G C F A 5fr

F C D A

C A F G 7fr

C A D F 6fr

G C F A 10fr

F C F A D 8fr

A G C F 12fr

F D A C 12fr

F

Fmaj7 (FM7)
F major seventh

F   A   C   E
root   3rd   5th   7th

F A C E

F C E A

5fr

F A C E

8fr

F C E A C

13fr

F   E A C

Fmaj9 (FM9)
F major ninth

F   A   C   E   G
root   3rd   5th   7th   9th

 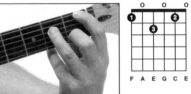

F A E G C E

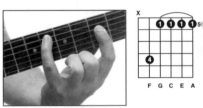

F A E G

5

F G C E A

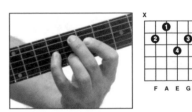

7

F A E G

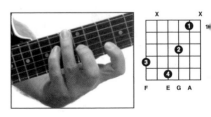

1

F   E G A

maj7#11 (FM7#11)
major seventh, sharp eleventh

F	A	C	E	B
root	3rd	5th	7th	#11th

Fm (Fmin, F-)
F minor

F	A♭	C
root	♭3rd	5th

F C E A B E

F C F A♭ C F

F B E A

3fr

F C F A♭

7fr

F A E A B

8fr

F C F A♭ C

8fr

F B E A C

9fr

A♭ C F A♭

12fr

F E A B

10fr

C A♭ C F

F

Fm(add 9)
F minor, added ninth

F	A♭	C	G
root	♭3rd	5th	9th

F A C G

A♭ G C F · 4fr

A♭ C F G · 8fr

A♭ C G C F · 10fr

F C F A♭ C G · 13fr

Fm6 (Fmin6, F-6)
F minor sixth

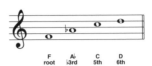

F	A♭	C	D
root	♭3rd	5th	6th

D A♭ C F

F C D A♭

F A♭ D F C

F D A♭ C

F C F A♭ D F

m7 (F-7, Fmin7)
minor seventh

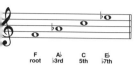

F	A♭	C	E♭
root	♭3rd	5th	♭7th

F C E♭ A♭ C F

X X
F C E♭ A♭

X
8fr
F C E♭ A♭ C

X X
9fr
C F A♭ E♭

X X
13fr
F E♭ A♭ C

Fm7♭5 (F-7♭5, Fmin7-5)
F minor seventh, flat fifth

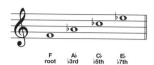

F	A♭	C♭	E♭
root	♭3rd	♭5th	♭7th

X X
F C♭ E♭ A♭

X X
4fr
E♭ A♭ C♭ F

X X
8fr
F C♭ E♭ A♭

X X
10fr
A♭ F C♭ E♭

X X
12fr
F E♭ A♭ C♭

F

Fm(maj7) (Fm(+7))
F minor, major seventh

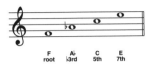

F A♭ C E
root ♭3rd 5th 7th

F C E A♭ C F

F C E A♭

F A♭ C E · 5fr

F C E A♭ C · 8fr

F E A♭ C · 13fr

Fm9 (F-9, Fmin9)
F minor ninth

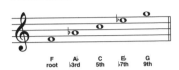

F A♭ C E♭ G
root ♭3rd 5th ♭7th 9th

F A♭ E♭ G

F A♭ E♭ G · 6fr

A♭ E♭ G C

A♭ G C E♭

F C E♭ A♭ C G

m11 (F-11, Fmin11)
minor eleventh

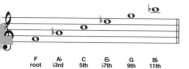

F	A♭	C	E♭	G	B♭
root	♭3rd	5th	♭7th	9th	11th

F7 (Fdom7)
F dominant seventh

F	A	C	E♭
root	3rd	5th	♭7th

F B♭ E♭ A♭ C G

F C E♭ A C F

F B♭ E♭ A♭

F C E♭ A

F A♭ E♭ G B♭ 6fr

E♭ C F A 5fr

F B♭ E♭ A♭ C 8fr

F C E♭ A C 8fr

F E♭ A♭ B♭ 11fr

C F A E♭ 10fr

F

F7sus4 (F7sus)
F dominant seventh, suspended fourth

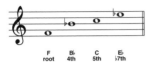

F root, Bb 4th, C 5th, Eb b7th

F C Eb Bb C F

F C Eb Bb   3fr

Eb C F Bb   5fr

F C Eb Bb C   8fr

C F Bb Eb   10fr

F7b5 (F7-5, Fdom7b5)
F dominant seventh, flat fifth

F root, A 3rd, Cb b5th, Eb b7th

Eb A Cb F

F Cb Eb A

Cb A Eb F

F Cb Eb A

F Eb A Cb

F   A   C   E♭   G
root 3rd 5th ♭7th 9th

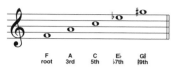

F7♯9 (F7+9, Fdom7♯9)
F dominant seventh, sharp ninth

F   A   C   E♭   G♯
root 3rd 5th ♭7th #9th

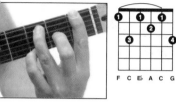

F C E♭ A C G

X X

F A   G♯

E♭

X X

F A E♭ G

X X

G♯   C   A

E♭

X

5fr

E♭ G C F A

X   X

7fr

F A E♭ G♯

X

7fr

F A E♭ G C

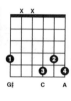

X

12fr

A E♭ G♯ C F

X   X

10fr

F   E♭ G A

13fr

F C E♭ A C G♯

F

F11
F eleventh

F root	A 3rd	C 5th	E♭ ♭7th	G 9th	B♭ 11th

F B♭ E♭ A C G

X X

F B♭ E♭ A

6fr

B♭ E♭ A E♭ F B♭

X

6fr

F A E♭ F B♭

X

8fr

F B♭ E♭ A C

F13 (Fdom13)
F thirteenth

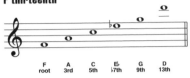

F root	A 3rd	C 5th	E♭ ♭7th	G 9th	D 13th

F C E♭ A D

X

E♭ A D F

X

F A E♭ G

X X

E♭ F A

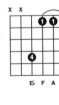

X

F E♭ A D

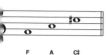

(Faug, F(♯5))
ugmented

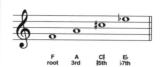

F+7 (F7♯5)
F dominant seventh, sharp fifth

F   A   C♯
root 3rd ♯5th

F A C♯ E♭
root 3rd ♯5th ♭7th

F A C♯ F

E♭ A C♯ F

4fr
C♯ C♯ F A

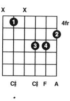

3fr
F C♯ E♭ A

6fr
F A C♯ F

6fr
E♭ A C♯ F

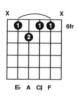

9fr
C♯ C♯ F A

8fr
F C♯ E♭ A C♯

10fr
C♯ F A F

13fr
F E♭ A C♯

83

F

F° (Fdim)
F diminished

F   Ab   Cb
root b3rd b5th

F Ab Cb F

Ab Ab Cb F 4fr

Ab Cb F Ab 4fr

Cb F Ab Cb 7fr

Ab Cb F Ab 9fr

F°7 (Fdim7)
F diminished seventh

F   Ab   Cb   Ebb
root b3rd b5th bb7th

F Cb Ebb A

Ebb Ab Cb F

F Cb Ebb Ab

Ab F Cb E

F Ebb Ab Cb

(F♯maj)
F-sharp major

F♯   A♯   C♯
root   3rd   5th

F♯5 (F♯ no 3rd)
F-sharp fifth (power chord)

F♯   C♯
root   5th

F♯ C♯ F♯ A♯ C♯ F♯

F♯ C♯ F♯

4fr

F♯ C♯ F♯ A♯

4fr

F♯ C♯ F♯

6fr

F♯ A♯ C♯ F♯

9fr

F♯ C♯ F♯

9fr

F♯ C♯ A♯

11fr

C♯ F♯ C♯ F♯

11fr

C♯ F♯ A♯ F♯

14fr

F♯ C♯ F♯

F#sus4 (F#sus)
F-sharp suspended fourth

F#   B   C#
root 4th 5th

F# C# F# B C# F#

X X
4fr
F# C# F# B

X   X
6fr
F# B C# F#

X   X
9fr
F# C# F# B

X X
11fr
C# F# B F#

F#sus2 (F#5add2)
F-sharp suspended second

F#   G#   C#
root 2nd 5th

X X

F#   G# C# F#

X X
F# C# F# G#

X
F# G# C# F#

X
F# C# F# G#

X X
C# G# C#

add9
harp added ninth

F♯	A♯	C♯	G♯
root	3rd	5th	9th

F♯6
F-sharp sixth

F♯	A♯	C♯	D♯
root	3rd	5th	6th

X X

F♯ A♯ C♯ G♯

X X

F♯ D♯ A♯ C♯

X X 6fr

G♯ C♯ F♯ A♯

X X 4fr

F♯ C♯ D♯ A♯

X 6fr

F♯ A♯ C♯ G♯ A♯

X X 7fr

C♯ A♯ D♯ F♯

F♯

X X 11fr

G♯ C♯ F♯ A♯

X 9fr

F♯ C♯ F♯ A♯ D♯

X X 13fr

A♯ G♯ C♯ F♯

X X 11fr

A♯ D♯ F♯ C♯

F#maj7 (F#M7)
F-sharp major seventh

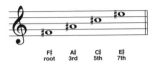

F#	A#	C#	E#
root	3rd	5th	7th

F#maj9 (F#M9)
F-sharp major ninth

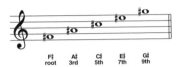

F#	A#	C#	E#	G#
root	3rd	5th	7th	9th

F# A# C# E#

F# A# E# G# C# F#

4fr

F# C# E# A#

F# A# E#

6fr

F# A# C# E#

F# G# C# E#

9fr

F# C# E# A# C#

F# A# E# G#

14fr

F# E# A# C#

G# C# F# A#

maj7♯11 (F♯M7♯11)
sharp major seventh, sharp eleventh

F♯	A♯	C♯	E♯	B♯
root	3rd	5th	7th	♯11th

F♯m (F♯-, F♯min)
F-sharp minor

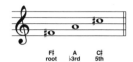

F♯	A	C♯
root	♭3rd	5th

F♯ A♯ E♯ A♯ B♯ E♯

F♯ C♯ F♯ A C♯ F♯

4fr

F♯ B♯ E♯ A♯

4fr

F♯ C♯ F♯ A

8fr

F♯ A♯ E♯ A♯ B♯

9fr

F♯ C♯ F♯ A C♯

9fr

F♯ B♯ E♯ A♯ C♯

10fr

A C♯ F♯ A

13fr

F♯ E♯ A♯ B♯

11fr

C♯ A C♯ F♯

F#m(add9)
F-sharp minor, added ninth

F#	A	C#	G#
root	b3rd	5th	9th

F# C# F# A C# G#

5fr

A   G# C# F#

10fr

G# C# F# A

11fr

A C# G# C# F#

14fr

F# A C# G#

F#m6 (F#-6, F#min6)
F-sharp minor sixth

F#	A	C#	D#
root	b3rd	5th	6th

F# C# F# A D# F#

F# C# D# A

F# A D# F# C#

F#   D# A C#

D# A C# F#

m7 (F♯–7, F♯min7)
sharp minor seventh

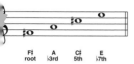

F♯	A	C♯	E
root	♭3rd	5th	♭7th

F♯m7♭5 (F♯–7♭5, F♯min7-5)
F-sharp minor seventh, flat fifth

F♯	A	C	E
root	♭3rd	♭5th	♭7th

F♯ C♯ E A C♯ F♯

F♯ E A C

4fr

F♯ C♯ E A

F♯ C E A

9fr

F♯ C♯ E A C♯

5fr

E A C F♯

F#

10fr

C♯ F♯ A E

9fr

F♯ C E A

14fr

F♯ E A C♯

11fr

A F♯ C E

F#m(maj7) (F#m(+7))
F-sharp minor, major seventh

F# A C# E#
root ♭3rd 5th 7th

F# C# E# A C# F#

X X   4fr

F# C# E# A

X   X   6fr

F# A C# E#

X   9fr

F# C# E# A C#

X   X   14fr

F#   E# A C#

F#m9 (F#-9, F#min9)
F-sharp minor ninth

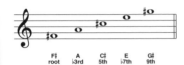

F# A C# E G#
root ♭3rd 5th ♭7th 9th

F# C# E A C# G#

X X

F# A E G

X   X

F# A E G#

X X

A E G# C#

X X

A   G# C# E

m11 (F#-11, F#min11)
harp minor eleventh

F# root	A ♭3rd	C# 5th	E ♭7th	G# 9th	B 11th

F#7 (F#dom7)
F-sharp dominant seventh

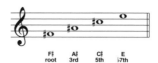

F# root	A# 3rd	C# 5th	E ♭7th

F# B E A C# G#

F# A# C# E

F# B E A

F# C# E A# C# F#

7fr

F# A E G# B

4fr

F# C# E A#

9fr

F# B E A C#

9fr

F# C# E A# C#

12fr

F# E A B

11fr

C# F# A# E

F#

F#7sus4 (F#7sus)
F-sharp dominant seventh, suspended fourth

F#	B	C#	E
root	4th	5th	♭7th

F#7♭5 (F#7-5, F#dom7♭5)
F-sharp dominant seventh, flat fifth

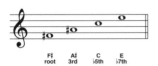

F#	A#	C	E
root	3rd	♭5th	♭7th

9
harp ninth

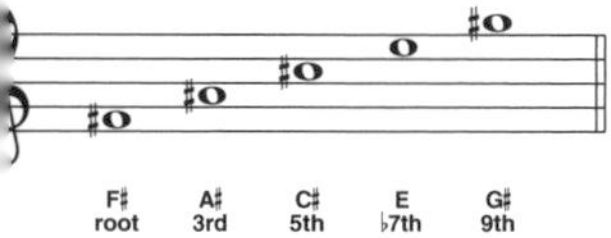

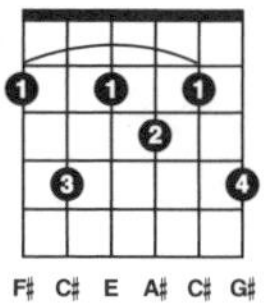

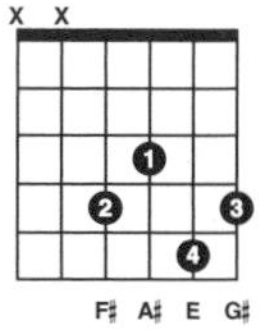

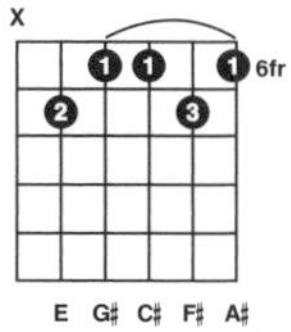

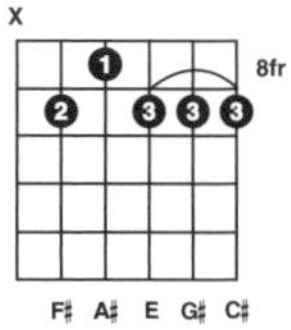

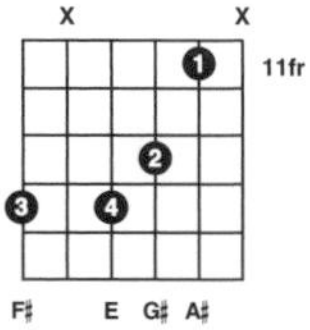

F♯7♯9 (F♯7+9, F♯dom7♯9)
F-sharp dominant seventh, sharp ninth

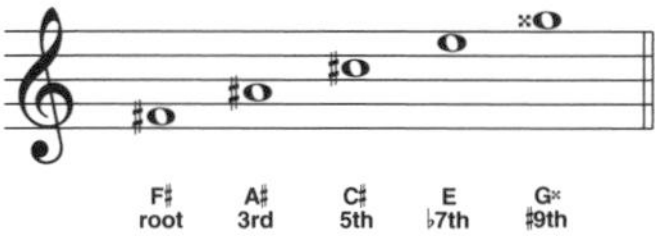

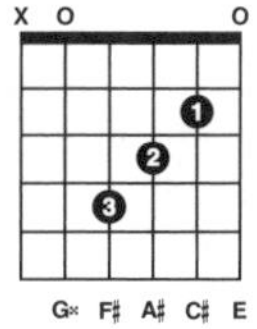

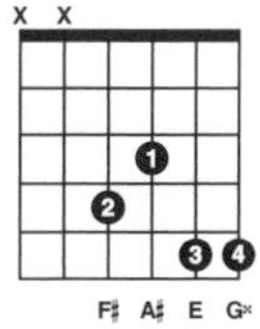

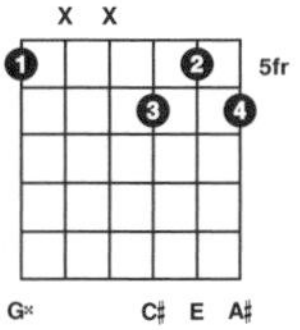

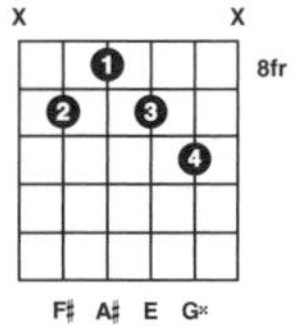

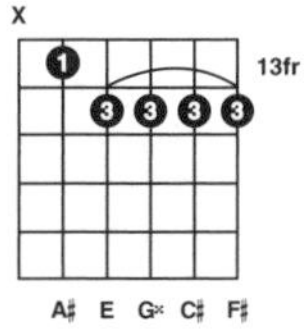

F#11
F-sharp eleventh

F#	A#	C#	E	G#	B
root	3rd	5th	♭7th	9th	11th

F#13 (F#dom13)
F-sharp thirteenth

F#	A#	C#	E	G#	D#
root	3rd	5th	♭7th	9th	13th

F# B E A# C# G#

F# C# E A# D# F#

F# B E A#

D# A# E F#

B E A# E F# B

E A# D# F#

F# A# E F# B

F# A# E G# D#

F# B E A# C#

F# E A# D#

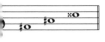 **+** (F#aug, F#(#5))
sharp augmented

F#+7 (F#7#5)
F-sharp dominant seventh, sharp fifth

F#   A#   C×
root 3rd   #5th

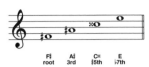

F#   A#   C×   E
root 3rd   #5th ♭7th

C× A# C× F#

F# A# C× E

5fr

C× C× F# A#

4fr

F# C× E A#

7fr

F# A# C× F#

7fr

E A# C× F#

10fr

C× C× F# A#

9fr

F# C× E A# C×

11fr

C× F# A# F#

14fr

F# E A# C×

F#

F#° (F#dim)
F-sharp diminished

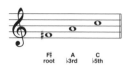

F#   A   C
root ♭3rd ♭5th

X X

F#   A C F#

X X

5fr

A C F# A

X X

8fr

C F# A C

X   X

10fr

A C F# A

X   X

13fr

C F# A C

F#°7 (F#dim7)
F-sharp diminished seventh

F#   A   C   E♭
root ♭3rd ♭5th ♭♭7th

O

F# A E♭ A C F#

X X

F# C E♭ A♭

X

F# C E♭ A C

X   X

A   F# C E♭

X   X

F#   E♭ A C

(Gmaj)
ajor

G   B   D
root 3rd 5th

G5 (G5 no 3rd)
G fifth (power chord)

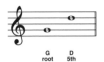

G   D
root 5th

o o o

G B D G B G

X X O O

D G D G

G D G B D G

X X O O

G D G

X X X

G D G

X X

G D G B

5fr

X X

G D G

5fr

X

X X

G B D G

7fr

X X X

G D G

10fr

X

X X

G D G B

10fr

X X

D G D G

12fr

G

Gsus4 (Gsus)
G suspended fourth

G — root
C — 4th
D — 5th

G C D G C G

G D G C D G

G D G C — 5fr

G C D G — 7fr

G D G C — 10fr

Gsus2 (G5add2)
G suspended second

G — root
A — 2nd
D — 5th

G A D A D G

G D G A

G A D G

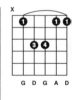
G D G A D

D A D G

dd9
dded ninth

G	B	D	A
root	3rd	5th	9th

G A D A B G

G B D A

A D G B 7fr

G B D A B 7fr

A D G B 12fr

G6
G sixth

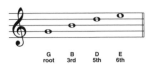

G	B	D	E
root	3rd	5th	6th

G B D G B E

G D E B 5fr

D B E G 8fr

G D G B E 10fr

G E B D 14fr

G

Gmaj7 (GM7)
G major seventh

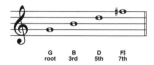

G	B	D	F♯
root	3rd	5th	7th

Gmaj9 (GM9)
G major ninth

G	B	D	F♯	A
root	3rd	5th	7th	9th

G B D G B F♯

G A D A B F♯

G F♯ B D

G B F♯ A♯

5fr

G D F♯ B

G A D F♯ B

7fr

G B D F♯

G B F♯ A

10fr

G D F♯ B D

A D G B F♯

maj7♯11 (GM7♯11)
major seventh, sharp eleventh

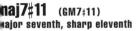

G	B	D	F♯	C♯
root	3rd	5th	7th	♯11th

Gm (G-, Gmin)
G minor

G	B♭	D
root	♭3rd	5th

o o

G B D G C♯ F♯

o o

G B♭ D G D G

X X

G F♯ B C♯

G D G B♭ D G

X X — 5fr

G C♯ F♯ B

X X — 5fr

G D G B♭

X — 9fr

G B F♯ B C♯

X — 10fr

G D G B♭ D

X — 10fr

G C♯ F♯ B D

X X — 12fr

D B♭ D G

G

Gm(add9)
G minor, added ninth

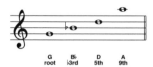

G	B♭	D	A
root	♭3rd	5th	9th

G D G B♭ D A

5fr

X X

B♭   D G A

6fr

X X

A D G B♭

11fr

X   X

A D G B♭

12fr

X

B♭ D A D G

Gm6 (G-6, Gmin6)
G minor sixth

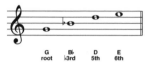

G	B♭	D	E
root	♭3rd	5th	6th

G B♭ D B♭ D E

G D G B♭ E G

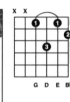

X X

G D E B♭

X

G B♭ E G D

X   X

G   E B♭ D

m7 (G-7, Gmin7)
minor seventh

G	B♭	·	D	F
root	♭3rd		5th	♭7th

Gm7♭5 (G-7♭5, Gmin7-5)
G minor seventh, flat fifth

G	B♭	D♭	F
root	♭3rd	♭5th	♭7th

G D F B♭ D G

G   F B♭ D♭

G   F B♭ D

5fr

G D♭ F B♭

5fr

G D F B♭

6fr

F B♭ D♭ G

G

10fr

G D F B♭ D

10fr

G D♭ F B♭

15fr

F B♭ D G

12fr

B♭   G D♭ F

Gm(maj7) (Gm(+7))
G minor, major seventh

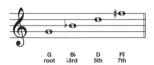

G	B♭	D	F♯
root	♭3rd	5th	7th

G D F♯ B♭ D G

G F♯ B♭ D

5fr
G D F♯ B♭

7fr
G B♭ D F♯

10fr
G D F♯ B♭ D

Gm9 (G-9, Gmin9)
G minor ninth

G	B♭	D	F	A
root	♭3rd	5th	♭7th	9th

G D F B♭ D A

G B♭ F A

G B♭ F A

B♭ F A D

B♭ A D F

m11 (G-11, Gmin11)
minor eleventh

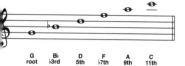

G	Bb	D	F	A	C
root	b3rd	5th	b7th	9th	11th

G7 (Gdom7)
G dominant seventh

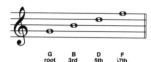

G	B	D	F
root	3rd	5th	b7th

G F Bb C

G B D G B F

G C F Bb D A

G D F B D G

5fr

G C F Bb

5fr

G D F B

8fr

G Bb F A C

10fr

G D F B D

10fr

G C F Bb D

12fr

D G B F

G

G7sus4 (G7sus)
G dominant seventh, suspended fourth

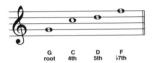

G root   C 4th   D 5th   F ♭7th

G C D G C F

G D F C D G

5fr

G D F C

10fr

G D F C D

12fr

D G C F

G7♭5 (G7-5, Gdom7♭5)
G dominant seventh, flat fifth

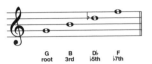

G root   B 3rd   D♭ ♭5th   F ♭7th

D♭ F G B F

G F B D♭

G D♭ F

D♭ F G

G D♭ F B

9
ninth

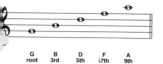

G	B	D	F	A
root	3rd	5th	♭7th	9th

G7#9 (G7+9, Gdom7#9)
G dominant seventh, sharp ninth

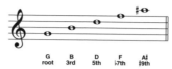

G	B	D	F	A#
root	3rd	5th	♭7th	#9th

O O O

② ①
③

G A D A B F

O O

①
②
③ ④

G B D A# B F

① ① ①
②
③ ④

G D F B D A

X X

① 4fr
②
③ ④

G B F A#

X X

① 4fr
②
③
④

G B F A

X X

① ② 6fr
③ ④

A# D F B

G

X

① 9fr
② ③ ③ ③

G B F A D

X X

① 9fr
② ③
④

G B F A#

X X

① 12fr
②
③ ④

G F A B

X

① 14fr
③ ③ ③ ③

B F A# D G

G11
G eleven

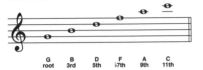

G	B	D	F	A	C
root	3rd	5th	♭7th	9th	11th

GBDACF

GCFBDA

GCFB

GBFGC

GCFBD

G13 (Gdom13)
G thirteenth

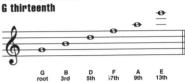

G	B	D	F	A	E
root	3rd	5th	♭7th	9th	13th

GAFABE

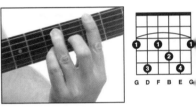

GDFBEG

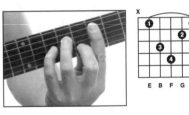

EBFGB

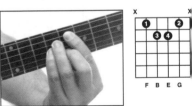

FBEG

GBFA

+ (Gaug, G(♯5))
augmented

G B D♯
root 3rd ♯5th

G+7 (G7♯5)
G dominant seventh, sharp fifth

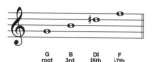

G B D♯ F
root 3rd ♯5th ♭7th

O O

G B D♯ G B G

X X O O

D♯ G B F

X X

G G B D♯

X

G F B D♯

X X 6fr

D♯ D♯ G B

X X 5fr

G D♯ F B

X X 8fr

G B D♯ G

X X 8fr

F B D♯ G

X X 12fr

D♯ G B G

X 10fr

G D♯ F B D♯

G

G° (Gdim)
G diminished

G root | B♭ ♭3rd | D♭ ♭5th

B♭ G D♭ G

B♭ D♭ G B♭ · 6fr

D♭ G B♭ D♭ · 9fr

B♭ D♭ G B♭ · 11fr

G B♭ D♭ G · 14fr

G°7 (Gdim7)
G diminished seventh

G root | B♭ ♭3rd | D♭ ♭5th | F♭ ♭♭7th

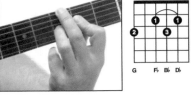

G F♭ B♭ D♭

D♭ B♭ F♭ G

G D♭ F♭ B♭

G D♭ F♭ B♭

F♭ G B♭ D♭

(A♭maj)
A♭ major

A♭ root   C 3rd   E♭ 5th

A♭5 (A♭ no 3rd)
A-flat fifth (power chord)

A♭ root   E♭ 5th

A♭ C E♭ A♭ C

E♭ A♭ E♭ A♭

4fr

A♭ E♭ A♭ C E♭ A♭

4fr

A♭ E♭ A♭

6fr

A♭ E♭ A♭ C

6fr

A♭ E♭ A♭

8fr

A♭ C E♭ A♭

11fr

A♭ E♭ A♭

A♭

11fr

A♭ E♭ A♭ C

13fr

E♭ A♭ E♭ A♭

A♭sus4 (A♭sus)
A-flat suspended fourth

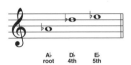

A♭ | D♭ | E♭
root | 4th | 5th

E♭ A♭ D♭ A♭

4fr
A♭ E♭ A♭ D♭ E♭ A♭

X X
6fr
A♭ E♭ A♭ D♭

X X
8fr
A♭ D♭ A♭

X X
11fr
A♭ E♭ A♭ D♭

A♭sus2 (A♭5add2)
A-flat suspended second

A♭ | B♭ | E♭
root | 2nd | 5th

X
B♭ E♭ A♭ E♭

X X
A♭ E♭ A♭

X
A♭ B♭ E♭ A♭

X
A♭ E♭ A♭ B♭

X
B♭ E♭ A♭ B♭

add9
at added ninth

A♭	C	E♭	B♭
root	3rd	5th	9th

A♭6
A-flat sixth

A♭	C	E♭	F
root	3rd	5th	6th

A♭ C E♭ B♭ C

A♭ C E♭ A♭ C F

4fr

A♭ C E♭ B♭

A♭ F C E♭

8fr

B♭ E♭ A♭ C

6fr

A♭ E♭ F C

8fr

A♭ C E♭ B♭

9fr

E♭ C F A♭

A♭

13fr

B♭ E♭ A♭ C

11fr

A♭ E♭ A♭ C F

A♭maj7 (A♭M7)
A-flat major seventh

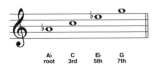

A♭	C	E♭	G
root	3rd	5th	7th

A♭maj9 (A♭M9)
A-flat major ninth

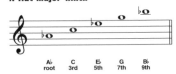

A♭	C	E♭	G	B♭
root	3rd	5th	7th	9th

♭maj7♯11 (A♭M7♯11)
♭at major seventh, sharp eleventh

A♭	C	E♭	G	D
root	3rd	5th	7th	♯11th

A♭m (A♭min, A♭-)
A-flat minor

A♭	C♭	E♭
root	♭3rd	5th

A♭

C E♭ A♭ D G

E♭ C♭ E♭ A♭

A♭ G C D

4fr

A♭ E♭ A♭ C♭ E♭ A♭

6fr

A♭ D G C

6fr

A♭ E♭ A♭ C♭

10fr

A♭ C G C D

11fr

A♭ E♭ A♭ C♭ E♭

11fr

A♭ D G C E♭

12fr

C♭ E♭ A♭ C♭

A♭m(add9)
A-flat minor, added ninth

A♭	C♭	E♭	B♭
root	♭3rd	5th	9th

C♭ E♭ B♭ E♭ A♭

4fr

A♭ E♭ A♭ C♭ E♭ B♭

6fr

C♭ E♭ A♭ B♭

7fr

B♭ E♭ A♭ C♭

12fr

B♭ E♭ A♭ C♭

A♭m6 (A♭min6, A♭-6)
A-flat minor sixth

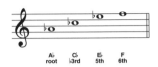

A♭	C♭	E♭	F
root	♭3rd	5th	6th

E♭ A♭ C♭

A♭ F C♭ E♭

A♭ E♭ A♭ C♭ F

A♭ E♭ F

A♭ C♭ F A♭

m7 (A♭-7, A♭min7)
at minor seventh

A♭	C♭	E♭	G♭
root	♭3rd	5th	♭7th

A♭m7♭5 (A♭-7♭5, A♭min7-5)
A-flat minor seventh, flat fifth

A♭	C♭	E♭♭	G♭
root	♭3rd	♭5th	♭7th

X   X

② ③ ③ ③

A♭ G♭ C♭ E♭

X   X

② ③ ④

A♭ G♭ C♭ E♭

① ① ① ① ① 4fr

③

A♭ E♭ G♭ C♭ E♭ A♭

X X

① 6fr

③ ③ ③

A♭ E♭ G♭ C♭

X X

① 6fr

② ③

④

A♭ E♭ G♭ C♭

X   X

① 7fr

② ③ ④

G♭ C♭ E♭♭ A♭

X X

① ① 9fr

③ ④

C♭ G♭ A♭ E♭

X   X

① ② 11fr

③ ④

A♭ E♭♭ G♭ C♭

A♭

X

① ① ① 11fr

②

③

A♭ E♭ G♭ C♭ E♭

X   X

① 13fr

② ③

④

C♭ A♭ E♭♭ G♭

A♭m(maj7) (A♭-(+7))
A-flat minor, major seventh

A♭	C♭	E♭	G
root	♭3rd	5th	7th

E♭ A♭ C♭ G

A♭ E♭ G C♭ E♭ A♭

A♭ E♭ G C♭

A♭ C♭ E♭ G

A♭ E♭ G C♭ E♭

A♭m9 (A♭-9, A♭min9)
A-flat minor ninth

A♭	C♭	E♭	G♭	B♭
root	♭3rd	5th	♭7th	9th

C♭ G♭ B♭ E♭

A♭ E♭ G♭ C♭ E♭

A♭ C♭ G♭

A♭ C♭ G♭ B♭

C♭ G♭ B♭

m11 (A♭-11, A♭min11)
at minor eleventh

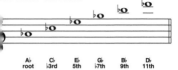

A♭	C♭	E♭	G♭	B♭	D♭
root	♭3rd	5th	♭7th	9th	11th

A♭7 (A♭dom7)
A-flat dominant seventh

A♭	C	E♭	G♭
root	3rd	5th	♭7th

A♭

A♭7sus4 (A♭7sus)
A-flat dominant seventh, suspended fourth

A♭	D♭	E♭	G♭
root	4th	5th	♭7th

E♭ A♭ D♭ G♭

4fr

A♭ E♭ G♭ D♭ E♭ A♭

6fr

A♭ E♭ G♭ D♭

9fr

E♭ D♭ G♭ A♭

11fr

A♭ E♭ G♭ D♭ E♭

A♭7♭5 (A♭7-5, A♭dom7♭5)
A-flat dominant seventh, flat fifth

A♭	C	E♭♭	G♭
root	3rd	♭5th	♭7th

E♭♭ A♭ C G♭

A♭ G♭ C E♭♭

A♭ E♭♭ G♭ C

E♭♭ G♭ A♭ C

A♭ E♭♭ G♭ C

9
...at ninth

A♭	C	E♭	G♭	B♭
root	3rd	5th	♭7th	9th

A♭7♯9 (A♭7+9, A♭dom7♯9)
A-flat dominant seventh, sharp ninth

A♭	C	E♭	G♭	B
root	3rd	5th	♭7th	♯9th

X   X

A♭   G♭ B♭ C

X

B E♭ A♭ C G♭

4fr

A♭ E♭ G♭ C E♭ B♭

X

C G♭ B E♭ A♭

X X   5fr

A♭ C G♭ B♭

X X   5fr

A♭ C G♭ B

X   8fr

G♭ B♭ E♭ A♭ C

X X   7fr

B   E♭ G♭ C

A♭

X   10fr

A♭ C G♭ B♭ E♭

X   X   10fr

A♭ C G♭ B

A♭11
A-flat eleventh

A♭	C	E♭	G♭	B♭	D♭
root	3rd	5th	♭7th	9th	11th

C E♭ A♭ D♭ G♭

A♭ D♭ G♭ C E♭ B♭ — 4fr

A♭ D♭ G♭ C — 6fr

A♭ C G♭ A♭ D♭ — 9fr

A♭ D♭ G♭ C E♭ — 11fr

A♭13 (A♭dom13)
A-flat thirteenth

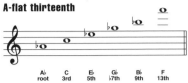

A♭	C	E♭	G♭	B♭	F
root	3rd	5th	♭7th	9th	13th

G♭ B♭ E♭ A♭ C

A♭ E♭ G♭ C F

F C G♭ A♭

G♭ C F A♭

A♭ C G♭ B♭

+ (A♭aug, A♭(♯5))
at augmented

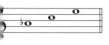

A♭   C   E
root   3rd   ♯5th

A♭+7 (A♭7♯5)
A-flat dominant seventh, sharp fifth

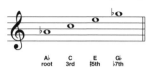

A♭   C   E   G♭
root   3rd   ♯5th   ♭7th

E C E A♭ C E

E C E A♭ C G♭

A♭   A♭ C E

4fr

A♭   G♭ C E

C E A♭ C

8fr

A♭ E G♭ C

6fr

A♭ C E A♭

9fr

G♭ C E A♭

9fr

A♭

E A♭ C A♭

13fr

A♭ E G♭ C E

11fr

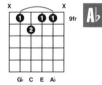

A♭° (A♭dim)
A-flat diminished

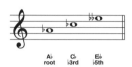

A♭	C♭	E♭♭
root	♭3rd	♭♭5th

X   O

C♭ E♭♭ A♭ E♭♭ A♭

X X

A♭   C♭ E♭♭ A♭

X X   7fr

C♭ E♭♭ A♭ C♭

X X   10fr

E♭♭ A♭ C♭ E♭♭

X   X 12fr

C♭ E♭♭ A♭ C♭

A♭°7 (A♭dim7)
A-flat diminished seventh

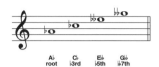

A♭	C♭	E♭♭	G♭♭
root	♭3rd	♭♭5th	♭♭7th

X X O   O

E♭♭ A♭ C♭ G♭♭

X   X

A♭ G♭♭ C♭ E♭♭

X X

A♭ E♭♭ G♭♭ C♭

X   X

A♭ E♭♭ G♭♭ C♭

X X

G♭♭   A♭ C♭ E♭♭

(Amaj)
ajor

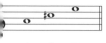

A   C♯   E
root   3rd   5th

A5 (A no 3rd)
A fifth (power chord)

A   E
root   5th

X O   O
A E A C♯ E

X O   X X
A E A

5fr
A E A C♯ E A

X O
A E A E A

X X   7fr
A E A C♯

X X X   5fr
A E A

X   X   9fr
A C♯ E A

X X   X   7fr
A E A

X   X   12fr
A E A C♯

X   X X   12fr
A E A

 127

A

Asus4 (Asus)
A suspended fourth

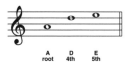

A · root | D · 4th | E · 5th

A E A D E

A E A D E A · 5fr

A E A D · 7fr

A D E A · 9fr

E A D A D E · 12fr

Asus2 (A5add2)
A suspended second

A · root | B · 2nd | E · 5th

A E A B

A B E

A E A

A B E A

B E A B

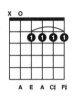

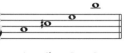

dd9
dded ninth

A — root
C# — 3rd
E — 5th
B — 9th

A E B C# E

A C# E B — 5fr

B E A C# — 9fr

A C# E B — 9fr

B E A C# — 14fr

A6
A sixth

A — root
C# — 3rd
E — 5th
F# — 6th

A E A C# F#

A F# C# E — 4fr

A E F# C# — 7fr

E C# F# A — 10fr

A E A C# F# — 12fr

A

Amaj7 (AM7)
A major seventh

A	C#	E	G#
root	3rd	5th	7th

A E G# C# E

A C# E G#

A G# C# E

A E G# C#

A C# E G#

Amaj9 (AM9)
A major ninth

A	C#	E	G#	B
root	3rd	5th	7th	9th

A E B C#

A C# G#

A B E G#

A C# G# B

B E A C#

aj7#11 (AM7#11)
ajor seventh, sharp eleventh

A	C#	E	G#	D#
root	3rd	5th	7th	#11th

Am (Amin, A-)
A minor

A	C	E
root	♭3rd	5th

A D# G# C# E

A E A C E

C# E A D# G#

A E A C E A   5fr

A G# C# D#   4fr

A E A C   7fr

A D# G# C#   7fr

A C E A   9fr

A C# G# C# D#   11fr

A E A C E   12fr

A

132

Am(add9)
A minor, added ninth

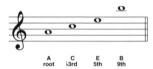

A root   C ♭3rd   E 5th   B 9th

A E B C E

5fr   A E A C E B

7fr   C E A B

8fr   B E A C

9fr   A C E B

Am6   (Amin6, A-6)
A minor sixth

A root   C ♭3rd   E 5th   F♯ 6th

A E A C F♯

A   F♯ C E

A E A C F♯ A

A E F♯ A

A C F♯ A

7 (A-7, Amin7)
inor seventh

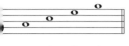

A   C   E   G
root   ♭3rd   5th   ♭7th

Am7♭5 (A-7♭5, Amin7♭5)
A minor seventh, flat fifth

A   C   E♭   G
root   ♭3rd   ♭5th   ♭7th

A E A C G

A E♭ A C G

A E G C E A   5fr

A   G C E♭

A E G C   7fr

A E♭ G C   7fr

A C G A E   10fr

G C E♭ A   8fr

A E G C E   12fr

A E♭ G C   12fr

A

Am(maj7) (A-(+7))
A minor, major seventh

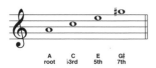

A root | C ♭3rd | E 5th | G♯ 7th

A E G♯ C E

A E G♯ C E A 5fr

A E G♯ C 7fr

A C E G♯ 9fr

A E G♯ C E 12fr

Am9 (A-9, Amin9)
A minor ninth

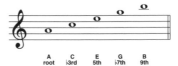

A root | C ♭3rd | E 5th | G ♭7th | B 9th

A C E G B

A E G C E 5fr

 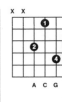

A C G 7fr

A C G B

C G B

11 (A-11, Amin11)
inor eleventh

A	C	E	G	B	D
root	♭3rd	5th	♭7th	9th	11th

A7 (Adom7)
A dominant seventh

A	C♯	E	G
root	3rd	5th	♭7th

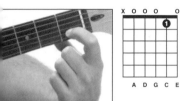

A D G C E

X O O O O

A E A C♯ G

X O

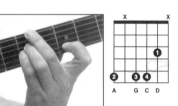

A G C D

X X

A E G C♯ E A

5fr

A D G C E B

5fr

A E G C♯

7fr

X X

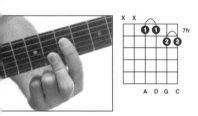

A D G C

7fr

X X

G E A C♯

9fr

X X

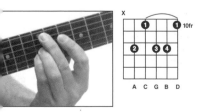

A C G B D

10fr

X

A E G C♯ E

12fr

X

A

A7sus4 (A7sus)
A dominant seventh, suspended fourth

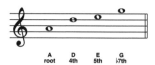

A
root

D
4th

E
5th

G
♭7th

A7♭5 (A7-5, Adom7♭5)
A dominant seventh, flat fifth

A
root

C♯
3rd

E♭
♭5th

G
♭7th

A E G D E

A E♭ A C♯

A E G D E A

A G C♯ E♭

A E G D

A E♭ G

D G A E

E♭ G A

A E G D E

A E♭ G C♯

nth

A	C♯	E	G	B
root	3rd	5th	♭7th	9th

A7♯9 (A7+9, Adom7♯9)
A dominant seventh, sharp ninth

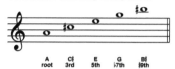

A	C♯	E	G	B♯
root	3rd	5th	♭7th	♯9th

A E B C♯ G

B♯ E A C♯ G

A G B C♯

C♯ G B♯ E A

5fr

A E G C♯ E B

6fr

A C♯ G B♯

6fr

A C♯ G B

8fr

B♯ E G C♯

11fr

A C♯ G B E

11fr

A C♯ G B♯

A

A11
A eleventh

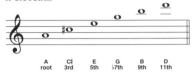

A	C#	E	G	B	D
root	3rd	5th	♭7th	9th	11th

A13 (Adom13)
A thirteenth

A	C#	E	G	B	F#
root	3rd	5th	♭7th	9th	13th

X O O O   O

A D G C# E

X O   O

A E G C# F#

1 1 1 1   5fr
    2
     3

A D G C# E B

1   1   1
  2
3   4

A E G C# F# A

X X
  1 1   7fr
   2
    3

A D G C#

X
1
  2
  3
  4

F# C# G A C

X
   1 1 10fr
  2
3   4

A C# G A D

X
1   2
  3 4

G C# F# A

X
1 1 1   1 12fr
    3

A D G C# E

X
  1
2   3 3

A C# G B

+ (Aaug, A(♯5))
ugmented

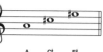

A   C♯   E♯
root   3rd   ♯5th

A+7 (A7♯5)
A dominant seventh, sharp fifth

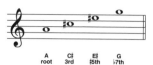

A   C♯   E♯   G
root   3rd   ♯5th   ♭7th

A E♯ A C♯ E♯

A E♯ G C♯ E♯

A   A C♯ E♯   5fr

A   G C♯ E♯   5fr

C♯ E♯ A C♯   9fr

A E♯ G C♯   7fr

A C♯ E♯ A   10fr

G C♯ E♯ A   10fr

A

C♯ E♯ A E♯   10fr

A E♯ G C♯   12fr

A° (Adim)
A diminished

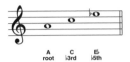

A root   C ♭3rd   E♭ ♭5th

X O   X

A E♭ A C

X   X

A   C E♭ A

X   X

8fr

C E♭ A C

X   X

11fr

E♭ A C E♭

X   X

13fr

C E♭ A C

A°7 (Adim7)
A diminished seventh

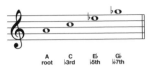

A root   C ♭3rd   E♭ ♭5th   G♭ ♭♭7th

X O

A E♭ A C G♭

X   X

A   G♭ C E♭

A E♭ A C G♭

X   X

A E♭ G♭

X

A E♭ G♭ C

(B♭maj)
...at major

B♭   D   F
root   3rd   5th

B♭5 (B♭ no 3rd)
B-flat fifth (power chord)

B♭   F
root   5th

X X O

D   B♭   D   F

X   X X

B♭   F   B♭

X   X

B♭   F   B♭   D

X X
3fr

F   B♭   F   B♭

6fr

B♭ F B♭ D F B♭

X X X
6fr

B♭   F   B♭

X X
8fr

B♭   F   B♭   D

X X   X
8fr

B♭   F   B♭

X   X
10fr

B♭   D   F   B♭

X X
13fr

F   B♭   F   B♭

B♭

B♭sus4 (B♭sus)
B-flat suspended fourth

B♭ E♭ F
root 4th 5th

X
① ①
② ③
④

B♭ F B♭ E♭ F

X X
① ① 3fr
②
④

F B♭ E♭ B♭

① ① ① 6fr
② ③ ④

B♭ F B♭ E♭ F B♭

X X
① 8fr
③
④ ④

B♭ F B♭ E♭

X X
① 10fr
②
③ ④

B♭ E♭ F B♭

B♭sus2 (B♭5add2)
B-flat suspended second

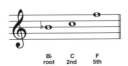

B♭ C F
root 2nd 5th

X
① ① ①
③ ④

B♭ F B♭ C F

X X
①
② ③ ④

B♭ C F B♭

X X
①
③
④

B♭ F B♭ C

X X
① ①
②
④

B♭ C F B♭

X X
①
② ③ ④

C F B♭ C

add9
at added ninth

Bb | D | F | C
root | 3rd | 5th | 9th

Bb6
B-flat sixth

Bb | D | F | G
root | 3rd | 5th | 6th

X

Bb F C D F

X O O

Bb D G D F

X   X

C F Bb D

3fr

Bb D F Bb D G

X X

6fr

Bb D F C

X   X

5fr

Bb   G D F

X X

10fr

C F Bb D

X X

8fr

Bb F G D

X   X

10fr

Bb D F C

X

13fr

Bb F Bb D G

Bb

143

B♭maj7 (B♭M7)
B-flat major seventh

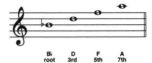

B♭ root	D 3rd	F 5th	A 7th

B♭ F A D F

B♭ D F A 5fr

B♭ A D F 6fr

B♭ F A D 8fr

B♭ D F A 10fr

B♭maj9 (B♭M9)
B-flat major ninth

B♭ root	D 3rd	F 5th	A 7th	C 9th

B♭ D A C

C F B♭ D

B♭ D A

B♭ C F A

B♭ D A C

naj7#11 (B♭M7#11)
t major seventh, sharp eleventh

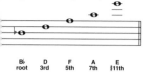

B♭	D	F	A	E
root	3rd	5th	7th	#11th

B♭m (B♭min, B♭-)
B-flat minor

B♭	D♭	F
root	♭3rd	5th

X · · · · O

B♭ F A D E

X

B♭ F B♭ D♭ F

X

D F B♭ E A

6fr

B♭ F B♭ D♭ F B♭

X · X · · 5fr

B♭ A D E

X · · · X 6fr

D♭ B♭ D♭ F

X X 8fr

B♭ E A D

X X 8fr

B♭ F B♭ D♭

X 12fr

B♭ D A D E

X · · · X 10fr

B♭ D♭ F B♭

B♭

B♭m(add9)
B-flat minor, added ninth

B♭	D♭	F	C
root	♭3rd	5th	9th

D♭ F B♭ C F

6fr

B♭ F B♭ D♭ F C

X X   8fr

D♭   F B♭ C

X X   9fr

C F B♭ D♭

X   X   10fr

B♭ D♭ F C

B♭m6 (B♭min6, B♭-6)
B-flat minor sixth

B♭	D♭	F	G
root	♭3rd	5th	6th

B♭ F G D♭

B♭ G D♭ F

B♭ F B♭ D♭ G

B♭ F G

B♭ D♭ G B♭

7 (B♭-7, B♭min7)
t minor seventh

B♭	D♭	F	A♭
root	♭3rd	5th	♭7th

B♭m7♭5 (B♭-7♭5, B♭min7♭5)
B-flat minor seventh, flat fifth

B♭	D♭	F♭	A♭
root	♭3rd	♭5th	♭7th

B♭ F A♭ D♭ F

B♭ F♭ A♭ D♭ F♭

6fr

B♭ A♭ D♭ F

5fr

B♭ A♭ D♭ F♭

6fr

B♭ F A♭ D♭ A♭ B♭

8fr

B♭ F♭ A♭ D♭

8fr

B♭ F A♭ D♭

9fr

A♭ D♭ F♭ B♭

11fr

B♭ D♭ A♭ B♭ F

13fr

B♭ F♭ A♭ D♭

B♭

B♭m(maj7) (B♭-(+7))
B-flat minor, major seventh

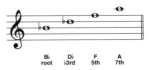

B♭ root / D♭ ♭3rd / F 5th / A 7th

B♭ F A D♭ F

B♭ F A D♭ F B♭ 6fr

B♭ F A D♭ 8fr

B♭ D♭ F A 10fr

B♭ A D♭ F 13fr

B♭m9 (B♭-9, B♭min9)
B-flat minor ninth

B♭ root / D♭ ♭3rd / F 5th / A♭ ♭7th / C 9th

D♭ F A♭ C

B♭ F A♭ D♭ F

B♭ D♭ A♭

B♭ D♭ A♭ C

D♭ A♭ C

n11 (B♭-11, B♭min11)
t minor eleventh

B♭ root	D♭ ♭3rd	F 5th	A♭ ♭7th	C 9th	E♭ 11th

B♭7 (B♭dom7)
B-flat dominant seventh

B♭ root	D 3rd	F 5th	A♭ ♭7th

B♭ E♭ A♭ D♭ F

B♭ F A♭ D F

4fr

B♭ A♭ D♭ E♭

F B♭ D A♭

6fr

B♭ E♭ A♭ D♭ F C

6fr

B♭ F A♭ D F B♭

8fr

B♭ E♭ A♭ D♭

8fr

B♭ F A♭ D

11fr

B♭ D♭ A♭ C E♭

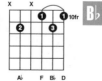

10fr

A♭ F B♭ D

B♭

B♭7sus4 (B♭7sus)
B-flat dominant seventh, suspended fourth

B♭ root | E♭ 4th | F 5th | A♭ ♭7th

B♭7♭5 (B♭7-5, B♭dom7♭5)
B-flat dominant seventh, flat fifth

B♭ root | D 3rd | F♭ ♭5th | A♭ ♭7th

t ninth

B♭	D	F	A♭	C
root	3rd	5th	♭7th	9th

B♭7♯9 (B♭7+9, B♭dom7♯9)
B-flat dominant seventh, sharp ninth

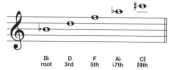

B♭	D	F	A♭	C♯
root	3rd	5th	♭7th	♯9th

B♭ D A♭ C F

B♭ D A♭ C♯ F

3fr

B♭ A♭ C D

5fr

D A♭ C♯ F B♭

6fr

B♭ F A♭ D F C

7fr

B♭ D A♭ C♯

7fr

B♭ D A♭ C

9fr

C♯ F A♭ D

12fr

B♭ D A♭ C F

12fr

B♭ D A♭ C♯

B♭

B♭11
B-flat eleventh

B♭ root	D 3rd	F 5th	A♭ ♭7th	C 9th	E♭ 11th

B♭13 (B♭dom13)
B-flat thirteenth

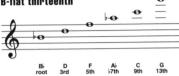

B♭ root	D 3rd	F 5th	A♭ ♭7th	C 9th	G 13th

B♭ E♭ A♭ D F

B♭ F A♭ D

6fr

B♭ E♭ A♭ D F C

B♭ F A♭ D G♭

8fr

B♭ E♭ A♭ D

G D A♭ B♭

9fr

D F A♭ E♭

A♭ D G E♭

11fr

B♭ D A♭ B♭ E♭

B♭ D A♭ G

+ (B♭aug, B♭(♯5))
at augmented

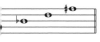

B♭   D   F♯
root   3rd   ♯5th

B♭+7 (B♭7♯5)
B-flat dominant seventh, sharp fifth

B♭   D   F♯   A♭
root   3rd   ♯5th   ♭7th

B♭ D B♭ D F♯

B♭ D A♭ D F♯

6fr

B♭ B♭ D F♯

B♭ F♯ A♭ D

6fr

B♭ D F♯ B♭

6fr

B♭ A♭ D F♯

7fr

B♭ D F♯ D

8fr

B♭ F♯ A♭ D

11fr

B♭ D F♯ B♭

11fr

A♭ D F♯ B♭

B♭

B♭° (B♭dim)
B-flat diminished

B♭   D♭   F♭
root   ♭3rd   ♭5th

B♭   F♭   B♭   D♭   F♭

D♭   F♭   B♭   D♭

B♭   D♭   F♭   B♭

D♭   F♭   B♭   D♭

F♭   B♭   D♭   F♭

B♭°7 (B♭dim7)
B-flat diminished seventh

B♭   D♭   F♭   A♭♭
root   ♭3rd   ♭5th   ♭♭7th

B♭   F♭   A♭♭   D♭

B♭   A♭♭   D♭   F♭

B♭   F♭   B♭   D♭   A♭♭

B♭   F♭   A♭♭

B♭   F♭   A♭♭   D♭

(Bmaj)
ajor

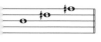

B   D♯   F♯
root   3rd   5th

B5 (B no 3rd)
B fifth (power chord)

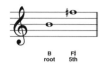

B   F♯
root   5th

B   F♯   B   D♯

B   F♯   B

4fr

B   D♯   F♯   D♯

4fr

F♯   B   F♯   B

7fr

B   F♯   B   D♯   F♯   B

7fr

B   F♯   B

9fr

B   F♯   B   D♯

9fr

B   F♯   B

11fr

B   D♯   F♯   B

14fr

B   F♯   B

B

Bsus4 (Bsus)
B suspended fourth

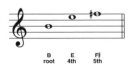

B E F#
root 4th 5th

X O O

B F# B B E

X X
4fr

F# B E B

7fr

B F# B E F# B

X X
9fr

B F# B E

X X
11fr

B E F# B

Bsus2 (B5add2)
B suspended second

B C# F#
root 2nd 5th

X

B F# B C#

X X

B C# F#

X X

B F# B

X

B C# F# B

X

C# F# B C#

d9
ded ninth

B	D#	F#	C
root	3rd	5th	9th

B6
B sixth

B	D#	F#	G#
root	3rd	5th	6th

C# F# B D#

B F# B D# G#

B F# C# D# F# 2fr

B D# F# B D# G# 4fr

B D# F# C# 7fr

B G# D# F# 6fr

C# F# B D# 11fr

B F# G# D# 9fr

B D# F# C# 11fr

B G# D# F# 13fr

B

Bmaj7 (BM7)
B major seventh

B	D♯	F♯	A♯
root	3rd	5th	7th

B F♯ A♯ D♯ F♯

6fr
B D♯ F♯ A♯

7fr
B A♯ D♯ F♯

9fr
B F♯ A♯ D♯

11fr
B D♯ F♯ A♯

Bmaj9 (BM9)
B major ninth

B	D♯	F♯	A♯	C♯
root	3rd	5th	7th	9th

B D♯ A♯ C♯

C♯ F♯ B D♯

B D♯ A♯ C♯ F♯

B D♯ A♯

B C♯ F♯ A♯

aj7#11 (BM7#11)
jor seventh, sharp eleventh

B	D#	F#	A#	E#
root	3rd	5th	7th	#11th

Bm (Bmin, B-)
B minor

B	D	F#
root	b3rd	5th

B D# A# D# E#

B F# B D F#

4fr

D# F# B E# A#

3fr

D F# B D

6fr

B A# D# E#

7fr

B F# B D F# B

9fr

B E# A# D#

9fr

B F# B D

11fr

D# F# A# E#

11fr

B D F# B

B

Bm(add9)
B minor, added ninth

B	D	F♯	C♯
root	♭3rd	5th	9th

Bm6 (Bmin6, B-6)
B minor sixth

B	D	F♯	G♯
root	♭3rd	5th	6th

n7 (B-7, Bmin7)
inor seventh

B D F♯ A
root ♭3rd 5th ♭7th

Bm7♭5 (B-7♭5, Bmin7♭5)
B minor seventh, flat fifth

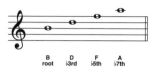

B D F A
root ♭3rd ♭5th ♭7th

B D A B F♯

B D A B F

B F♯ A D F♯

B F A D

B A D F♯ 7fr

B A D F 6fr

B F♯ A D A B 7fr

B F A D 9fr

B F♯ A D 9fr

B D F A 10fr

B

Bm(maj7) (B-(+7))
B minor, major seventh

B root / D ♭3rd / F♯ 5th / A♯ 7th

Bm9 (B-9, Bmin9)
B minor ninth

B root / D ♭3rd / F♯ 5th / A ♭7th / C♯ 9th

11 (B-11, Bmin11)
nor eleventh

B	D	F♯	A	C♯	E
root	♭3rd	5th	♭7th	9th	11th

B7 (Bdom7)
B dominant seventh

B	D♯	F♯	A
root	3rd	5th	♭7th

B D A C♯ E

B D♯ A B F♯

B E A D F♯

B F♯ A D♯ F♯

5fr

B A D E

7fr

B F♯ A D♯ F♯ B

7fr

B E A D F♯ C♯

9fr

B F♯ A D♯

9fr

B E A D

11fr

A F♯ B D♯

B7sus4 (B7sus)
B dominant seventh, suspended fourth

B	E	F#	A
root	4th	5th	♭7th

X   O

B E A B F#

X

B F# A E F#

7fr

B F# A E F# B

X X   9fr

B F# A E

X X   12fr

E A B F#

B7♭5 (B7-5, Bdom7♭5)
B dominant seventh, flat fifth

B	D#	F	A
root	3rd	♭5th	♭7th

X O   O

A D# A B

X

B F A D#

 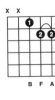

X

B A D# F

X X

B F A

X X

F A B

…th

B	D#	F#	A	C#
root	3rd	5th	♭7th	9th

B7#9 (B7+9, Bdom7#9)
B dominant seventh, sharp ninth

B	D#	F#	A	C✕
root	3rd	5th	♭7th	#9th

B D# A C# F#

B D# A C✕

B A C# D#

C✕ F# B D# A

B F# A D# F# C#

D# A C✕ F# B

B D# A C#

B D# A C✕

B D# A C#

C✕ F# A D#

B

B11
B eleventh

B	D♯	F♯	A	C♯	E
root	3rd	5th	♭7th	9th	11th

B D♯ A C♯ E

B E A D♯ F♯

B E A D♯ F♯ C♯ — 7fr

B E A D♯ — 9fr

B D♯ A B E — 12fr

B13
B thirteenth

B	D♯	F♯	A	C♯	G♯
root	3rd	5th	♭7th	9th	13th

B D♯ A C♯

B F♯ A D♯

B F♯ A D♯ G♯

G♯ D♯ A B

A D♯ G♯ B

(Baug, B(♯5))
ugmented

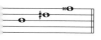

B · D♯ · F×
root · 3rd · ♯5th

B+7 (B7♯5)
B dominant seventh, sharp fifth

B · D♯ · F× · A
root · 3rd · ♯5th · ♭7th

X · O · O

B · D♯ · F× · B · F×

X · O

B · D♯ · A · B · F×

X · X · 7fr

B · B · D♯ · F×

X · X

B · F× · A · D♯

X · X · 7fr

B · D♯ · F× · B

X · X · 7fr

B · A · D♯ · F×

X · X · 8fr

B · D♯ · F× · D♯

X · X · 9fr

B · F× · A · D♯

X · X · 12fr

B · D♯ · F× · B

X · X · 12fr

A · D♯ · F× · B

B

B° (Bdim)
B diminished

B root   D ♭3rd   F ♭5th

B D B D F

B F B D

6fr

B   D F B

10fr

D F B D

13fr

F B D F

B°7 (Bdim7)
B diminished seventh

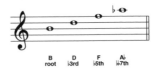

B root   D ♭3rd   F ♭5th   A♭ ♭♭7th

B F A♭ D

B   A♭ D F

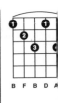

B F B D A♭

B F A♭

B F A♭